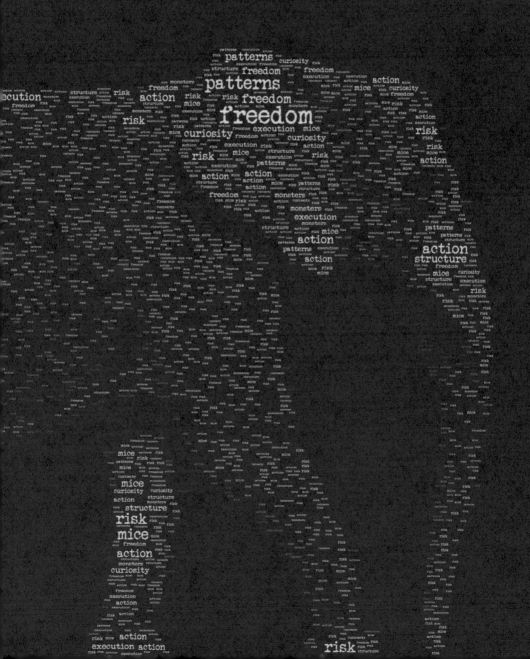

LET *the* ELEPHANTS RUN

UNLOCK YOUR CREATIVITY AND CHANGE EVERYTHING

DAVID USHER

LET *the* ELEPHANTS RUN

UNLOCK YOUR CREATIVITY AND CHANGE EVERYTHING

ANANSI

This edition published in 2015 by
House of Anansi Press Inc.
110 Spadina Avenue, Suite 801
Toronto, ON, M5V 2K4
T 416 363 4343 / F 416 363 1017
houseofanansi.com

Distributed in Canada by
HarperCollins Canada Ltd.
1995 Markham Road
Scarborough, ON, M1B 5M8
Toll free tel.
1 800 387 0117

Distributed in the United States by
Publishers Group West
1700 Fourth Street
Berkeley, CA 94710
Toll free tel.
1 800 788 3123

Printed on Stora Multifine Woodfree paper derived from sustainable sources

19 18 17 16 15   1 2 3 4 5

Library and Archives Canada Cataloguing in Publication

Usher, David, author
Let the elephants run : unlock your creativity and change everything
/ by David Usher.

Issued in print and electronic formats.
ISBN 978-1-77089-868-4 (bound). – ISBN 978-1-77089-869-1 (html)

1. Creative ability. 2. Usher, David – Anecdotes. I. Title.

BF408.U74 2015   153.3'5   C2014-906114-5
                                                     C2014-906115-3

Library of Congress Control Number: 2014949817

Graphic design: Caroline Blanchette
Cover design: Alysia Shewchuk
Art direction: Caroline Blanchette and David Usher
Cover image: detail from "Breathe" illustration by Craig Kirkham

*We acknowledge for their financial support of our publishing program
the Canada Council for the Arts, the Ontario Arts Council, and
the Government of Canada through the Canada Book Fund.*

Printed and bound in Singapore

For OCÉANE, COCO, and SABRINA

CONTENTS

INTRODUCTION   5

PART ONE FREEDOM   33

PART TWO STRUCTURE   116

CONCLUSION   216

ACKNOWLEDGEMENTS   221

CREDITS QUOTES   222

CREDITS PHOTOS   224

RULE NUMBER ONE
Never start a serious book with a photo of yourself
standing in your underwear.

RULE NUMBER TWO
In the land of creativity there are no rules...

THIS IS THE THREE-YEAR-OLD ME. THIS PERSON, STANDING POISED WITH A BOW AND ARROW — WEARING NOTHING BUT HIS UNDERWEAR — HOLDS THE KEYS TO CREATIVITY. HE HAS ENDLESS CURIOSITY AND LIMITLESS IMAGINATION. HE ASKS A MILLION QUESTIONS AND LOVES TO LEARN. HE IS A SPONGE TO THE WORLD AND AN OPEN RECEPTOR TO ALL THE AMAZING IDEAS AROUND HIM. THIS IS THE "ME" I MUST ACCESS TO HAVE A DYNAMIC CREATIVE PROCESS. *But LIFE changes us.*

the WORK

the DRAMA

the BOOZE

the DISHES

the MORTGAGE

the KIDS

the BILLS

the WORK

the DRAMA

the BOOZE

the DISHES

the MORTGAGE

the KIDS

the BILLS

the WORK

the DRAMA

the BOOZE

the DISHES

the MORTGAGE

the KIDS

the BILLS

the WORK

the DRAMA

the BOOZE

the DISHES

the MORTGAGE

the KIDS

Layer upon layer of life begins to separate us from our child's mind. We become experts at our jobs and we become more experienced. We shut ourselves off and focus on the "important things." Slowly, over time, we forget to be curious, to keep learning, to imagine — and maybe our dreams begin to fade a bit.

But the child's mind still exists. It's somewhere near the back of our heads, waiting just below the surface. If you spend a little time searching, you can still find that person; it is still possible to reconnect with your curiosity and wonder. To be more creative, you need to find this version of "you": the person who can still imagine the impossible.

For as long as I can remember, I have loved making things. One of my earliest memories is of driving with my family across Canada to Nova Scotia on holiday. I was four years old and I spent the entire trip standing on the hump between the two front seats, one hand on each, making up songs about anything we passed on the highway and singing them at the top of my lungs. This was in the era before seatbelt laws, or even seatbelt awareness. "The horsey in the barn, he could be on the left" was one of my first hits. That burning desire to sing and write songs has stayed with me for my entire life. I have a great career in music and it has allowed me to tour all over the world and meet some incredible people. Music has been very good to me, but the creative bug that started with songwriting has led me to work in all kinds of creative disciplines: music, technology, consulting, speaking, entrepreneurship, and activism. To some that might sound like an unmanageable, dizzying number of areas in which to live, but for me, it just works. And the reason is clear: beneath the surface, the creative process utilized by all of these different disciplines is remarkably similar. Once you identify and engage these essential elements of the process, the rest is simple. When you start to see creative thinking as independent of genre or discipline, suddenly you can work on almost anything.

There is something magical, almost indescribable, that happens in the moment of creation — the moment of bliss, surprise, and wonder when all forces of the universe come into focus for just a split second. Suddenly, you can see something that no one else can see. It's like a drug, really. Once you've tasted it, you can never turn away, and you find yourself continually trying to recapture that feeling.

This book is about getting to that moment. Not by luck or magic, but by stripping away the myths that surround the creative process and tackling the work and discipline that it really takes to get there. Popular myth would have us believe that a few people are born creative while the rest are not. It's much easier to believe in magic than in work, or in divinity than in struggle. But look a little closer and you will find that creativity is an intrinsic part of being human, and it is written into every person's DNA. Many people live their lives oblivious to and alienated from their inherent creative nature. Creativity is not just magic; it is a learnable skill that any person or company can acquire. I have spent my life refining that process, and I can tell you that it really is possible to reconnect with your creative self. You just have to take the time, make the commitment, and learn how. Within creative thinking lives the power of transformation. It can create objects, change habits, and transform people. Through creativity you can change everything.

ACTION

Throughout this book are small tasks designed to put your ideas in motion. The trick to learning the skill of creativity and creative thinking is through action. This is not a passive sport. Only through actions will you actually be able to reignite your creativity.

A WORLD WITHOUT

Look around you, wherever you are. Take it all in. The sights, the sounds. Now imagine a world without creativity. First, let's take away music. All the music. The heavy metal you loved in your teens and the pop music you listen to on the radio at work. Now let's take away dance and theatre. Poof! Gone! The art, paintings, sculptures, and drawings. Subtract movies, all the great TV shows, and video games. But it doesn't stop there. Let's take away writing: the books, magazines, articles, blogs — all the things you love to read. Then the spoken word, the ability to formulate sentences and complex thoughts, all language. Now move to the world of things. Start with your computer, your fridge, the medicine you give your kids, the clothes you wear, the car you drive, and the house you live in. Then the infrastructure starts to disappear. The roads, the bridges, the heating, the buildings, the power grid, and, finally, the very floor you are standing on.

CREATIVITY

WHAT'S LEFT?

JUST YOU!

Naked, sitting in an empty field. It's dark and the grass is wet against your bare skin. Something big is moving in the bushes just beyond the ridge. Better get up — and start running.

ACTION

ONE

Start simple. Get a pencil or pen.

I want you to write in this book. To get your creativity flowing you need to start taking notes and collecting ideas about the world around you. This is the first step of any creative process. Learning to be creative is itself a creative act. Every time you pick up this book be prepared to write, scribble in the margins about anything that sparks your interest. Start cultivating the habit of documenting ideas. Use this book as a simple starting point.

Throughout our lives most of us have been taught
not to write in books and mess up the pages.
I want you to do the opposite. Break the seal.
Write, draw, scribble on the page below...

The CREATIVE APE

Approximately 3.6 million years ago this happy couple walked naked across the plains of Africa. Like most of their bipedal hominid relations that followed, they were blissfully unaware of their impending extinction. Flash forward and, years later, human beings would narrowly escape the same fate. In the study "The Dawn of Human Matrilineal Diversity," Dr. Spencer Wells, the director of the Genographic Project, outlined the theory that a mere 70,000 years ago, after decades of climate change, drought, and struggle, humanity had been reduced to as few as 2,000 individuals on the verge of extinction. He described it as a moment in history when the fate of humanity balanced on a razor's edge: "Tiny bands of early humans, forced apart by harsh environmental conditions, [came] back from the brink to reunite and populate the world. Truly an epic drama."

Somehow, from the edge, we made a comeback.

How did we do it? We have no natural defences. We have no fur to protect us against the cold, no claws to take down prey. We can't really run fast or jump particularly high. We can't fly or spit poison. Our babies are born useless and vulnerable, unable even to walk for the first year. We are defenceless, except for one thing: our really big brains. Within our brains lives the key to our great competitive advantage, an advantage that has allowed us to grow from a population of 2,000 to 7 billion. It has enabled us to become the dominant species on earth, pushing the limits of our planet and even our solar system. Somewhere deep in our grey matter a switch turned on and a connection was made. We have something that almost no other creature on earth can emulate: the ability to bring multiple disparate ideas together and make something completely new. We have what I call "the creative gene." Every man-made thing we use throughout the day has been based on that one ability: the ability to be creative.

BUT *i am* NOT CREATIVE

During a particularly long layover at Heathrow Airport a woman came running up to me. "David, I just love your song 'St. Lawrence River.'" She was very excited, and we got into a long, in-depth conversation about the meaning of the song. In our conversation, she said those words that I hear all the time: "I would love to write something like that, but I'm just not creative." Of course I was flattered, but at the same time, those words drive me absolutely crazy. To me, the statement "I am not creative" implies that creativity is something you're either born with, or you're not. As though I sit down at the piano, crack open a bottle of whiskey, wait patiently for divine intervention to hit me on the head like a hammer, and then the songs come pouring out fully formed like popcorn or bubbles. Believe me, I wish that were true, but the reality is that creativity is 95 percent work and discipline, and just 5 percent inspiration. You never get to the 5 percent inspiration that you desperately want and need unless you do the 95 percent that's work. I spent a year writing "St. Lawrence River," and I probably wrote thirty different choruses for it before I found the right one to record. The simple fact is that we are not taught or encouraged to exercise our creative muscles. In reality, we are encouraged to suppress them. This does not mean that most of us are not creative, only that we have never been trained to work on and value our creativity and imagination. When was the last time you invested time in developing your creativity?

Listen to the song **"ST. LAWRENCE RIVER"** *at* lettheelephantsrun.com

STOP
LOOKING AT
CREATIVITY
AS THE LOTTERY
THAT SOMEONE
ELSE WON
AT BIRTH.

START

LOOKING AT
CREATIVE THINKING
AS A SKILL SET THAT
YOU CAN MASTER
IF YOU INVEST
THE TIME
TO LEARN HOW.

ACTION

~~~~~~~~~~~~~~~~~~~~~~~~~~~~~~~~~~~~

TWO

To start to change and/or reset our creative thinking we first need to begin by analyzing it. Fill in the following survey about your own creativity.

MY CREATIVITY IS A... **1 2 3 4 5 6 7 8 9 10**

WHEN I WAS YOUNG MY CREATIVITY WAS A... **1 2 3 4 5 6 7 8 9 10**

I LOVE NEW EXPERIENCES **1 2 3 4 5 6 7 8 9 10**

I USED TO LOVE NEW EXPERIENCES **1 2 3 4 5 6 7 8 9 10**

PEOPLE CONSIDER ME OPEN-MINDED **1 2 3 4 5 6 7 8 9 10**

WHEN I WAS YOUNG I LOVED TO MAKE _____

I _*never*_ STOPPED BECAUSE _____

I AM COMFORTABLE WITH PEN AND PAPER ⬡
COMPUTERS AND TECHNOLOGY ⬡

I WRITE. **YES / NO**

I KEEP A JOURNAL. ⬡

I BLOG. ⬡

I READ. **YES / NO**
FICTION ⬡ **NON-FICTION** ⬡ **POETRY** ⬡

I DREAM. **YES / NO**

I DREAM IN COLOUR. **YES / NO / MAYBE**

I REMEMBER MY DREAMS. **YES / NO / SOMETIMES**

I AM A GOOD LEADER. **YES / NO**
WHY? _____

I AM A NERVOUS PERSON. **YES / NO**
WHY? _____

I AM COMFORTABLE SPEAKING IN FRONT OF GROUPS. **YES / NO**

I SEE THE WORLD IN
COLOURS / SHAPES / NUMBERS / WORK / PEOPLE / RELATIONSHIPS / EMOTIONS

I WORK **ALONE / WITH PEOPLE**

I WANT TO WORK **ALONE / WITH PEOPLE**

MY LAST CREATIVE PROJECT WAS _____

I CONSIDER IT A **SUCCESS / FAILURE**
WHY? _____

BEYOND *the* WORLD OF THINGS

Once you start to look at the world through the lens of creativity, everything looks different. Creative thinking is an integral part of everything we make, but also every relationship we have and every interaction in our lives. It's not just about the world of things. It exists in the connections we make, how we formulate sentences, the way we negotiate with our bosses, and how we choose to look at the world. Once you see the creative process as the underpinning of all these connections and interactions, then the world really is different. Instead of just acting by instinct and routine, repeating the same patterns over and over, you begin to view interactions as possibilities, and you can become an active participant. Every moment and interaction becomes an opportunity to apply the principles of creative thinking.

In Roger Fisher's classic book, *Getting to Yes*, he outlines how so many of our everyday interactions are really creative negotiations. "You negotiate with your spouse about where to go for dinner and with your child about when the lights go out. Negotiation is a basic means of getting what you want from others. It is back-and-forth communication designed to reach an agreement when you and the other side have some interests that are shared and others that are opposed." Each one of these interactions is an exercise in the creative process. We tend to naturally fall back to our instinctual patterns. "Inventing options does not come naturally. Not inventing is the normal state of affairs, even when you are outside a stressful negotiation."

"The eagles who soar through the sky are at rest and the creatures who crawl, run and creep. I know you're not thirsty. That's bullshit. Stop lying. Lie the fuck down, My darling, and sleep."

ADAM MANSBACH *Go the f*** to sleep*

I am always amazed when I see people who are incredibly gifted in their one creative discipline but then completely clueless and dumbfounded by all other parts of their lives. They have a highly developed creative process in one area but it is completely one-dimensional. They can only engage their creative thinking in relation to one thing: their chosen discipline. They are unable to recognize and extract the principles and processes that make them so successful and apply those same principles to other areas in their lives.

The opportunities to implement the principles of the creative process are everywhere. Once you start to recognize these interactions as creative opportunities, then every interaction you have becomes an opportunity to exercise your creative thinking and change the outcome. Creativity becomes much broader than the world of "things," and the opportunities to use your creative thinking become infinite.

ACTION

THREE

When was the last time you used the power of your creativity to influence the course of your life? Was it today, yesterday, or was it years ago? If you could reconnect with your creative self, what would you change? Creative thinking is transformative. Make a list of all the things you would change in your life if you could. Every creative process starts with the smallest action. Don't hold back; it's not a test. Just start writing.

What are the...

Things you would love to make?

Habits you would like to alter?

Relationships you wish were different?

FREAKS
&GEEKS

I love being an artist. I really do. But the reality is that I am only half artist, and the other half is geek. This means that, like most artists, I have a romantic vision of the creative process. I love to think about following my muse, and about how I was struck by a unique magical moment of genius at three in the morning, pouring my thoughts out in my notebook while draining the last drops of a bottle of Lagavulin. The artist in me loves the myth of the artist: the bohemian, the wild and free mind that lives and works outside the status quo. I'll admit it: I grew up wanting to be a character in Ernest Hemingway's *A Moveable Feast*.

The geek in me likes to look at the data. He wants to strip away the trappings of the process and look at what is actually happening, quantify it all, and then figure out how to do it again but more efficiently. How did I actually get to that moment at 3 a.m.? What was really going on, and how can I do it over and over again and be able to hit that elusive moment of creative elation more frequently? The geek in me wants to break it down and chart it out.

For my creativity to function I need to engage both sides of myself: the freak and the geek.

"But Paris was a very old city and we were young and nothing was simple there, not even poverty, nor sudden money, nor the moonlight, nor right and wrong nor the breathing of someone who lay beside you in the moonlight."

ERNEST HEMINGWAY *A Moveable Feast*

A LEARNABLE
Skill

Creativity isn't elitist. It's not just for "special people." Creativity is a learnable skill, and something that anyone who is willing to invest the time can achieve. You can learn to speak French. You can learn to drive a car. You can learn to write songs, learn to paint, learn to design, learn to be an entrepreneur. You can also learn the steps of the creative process and creative thinking. It really is no different. Some will be more naturally talented at specific creative disciplines than others, but determination and grit mean as much, if not more, than natural talent.

It's easier to believe in divine anointment than in the endless grind. It's easier to believe in talent than in work and discipline. Want to be really good at playing the piano? Try practising every day, for four hours a day, and then do that for four years. I guarantee that you'll be pretty damn good, and I can assure you that every eight-to-fourteen-year-old child who applies for the Music Advancement Program at Juilliard does at least that much practising. That's why they are so damn good.

Like everything in life, you still need a bit of luck and timing for it all to come together. But creativity itself — the ability to think of an innovative idea and then follow through with the steps of the process and deliver something new — is something we can all learn to do.

For creativity to work we need to harness the power of two seemingly opposing forces simultaneously.

FREEDOM & STRUCTURE

These are the keys we must find and master to make creativity happen. We need freedom of imagination in order to be curious, to explore, and to dream up bold ideas. At the same time, we also need a defined and disciplined structure — a methodology to the madness that, when applied, can make those imagined ideas a reality. Think of freedom as the skin and structure as the bones. You need both to stay alive. Freedom without structure is just chaos, and great ideas float away on the wind. But it all begins with freedom of imagination. To think creatively, you first need to get your imagination firing again...

Dear Imagination

It's been a long cold win
and you have been asleep
to long.
I have missed you.
It's time to wake the he
up and get back
to work.

by
COCO USHER
AGE 7

The CHILD'S MIND

I have young kids, so the experience is fresh for me. When you walk into a good and loving preschool what you see is imagination gone wild: crazy, excited play and boundless creativity. There are kids in one corner riding imaginary horses, others with their hands deep in paint making incredible art. Some are running for cover from descending dragons, or wiggling on the floor as mermaids in an undersea world. They are all doing something creative. If you give children freedom, they naturally know how to play. What you will not see (if you give them that freedom) is half the kids playing while the other half sit like lumps waiting for instructions on what to do. Children instinctively know how to use their imaginations, how to be creative, and how to let it all hang out. It is as natural as breathing.

We don't need to teach children to be creative; in fact, most of the time we just need to get out of the way. Openness and the ability to access exploratory play are big parts of creativity, but as we get older we become alienated from these abilities. We were all born with this built-in imagination. That is, until the organizational efficiencies of the school system drive it out of us.

THREE-YEAR-OLDS ON CHRISTMAS MORNING. THEY OPEN THEIR PRESENTS AND THEN PLAY WITH THE BOXES.

In a study published in the science journal *Cognition*, MIT professor Laura Schulz and her colleagues looked at how four-year-olds learn. She took a toy — consisting of four tubes that could be played with in a number of different ways — and gave it to two different groups of children. She let the first group discover the toy's many functions on their own. With the second group she acted more like a teacher, instructing them on how the toy worked but only in one specific way. Then she left both groups of children alone to play with the toy. As Alison Gopnik described in Slate:

"All of the children pulled the first tube to make it squeak. The question was whether they would also learn about the other things the toy could do. The children from the first group played with the toy longer and discovered more of its 'hidden' features than those in the second group. In other words, direct instruction made the children less curious and less likely to discover new information."

Throughout our lives, the more we "learn," the easier it is to become disconnected from our childlike curiosity. To restart our creativity we need to reconnect to our natural ability for exploratory play.

"There's probably no better example of the throttling of creativity than the difference between what we observe in a kindergarten classroom and what we observe in a high school classroom... Take a room full of five-year-olds and you will see creativity in all its forms positively flowing around the room. A decade later you will see these same children passively sitting at their desks, half asleep or trying to decipher what will be on the next test."

MADELINE LEVINE *Teach Your Children Well*

ACTION

FOUR

Find a few photographs of yourself when you were a kid, four or five years old. Glue one into this book on the opposite page, put the second on your bedside table so you can see it when you wake up, and place another one in the space where you work. This is the person you need to find. This is the reminder that your imagination still exists. You are still a creative being who can dream up amazing things. You're just a little rusty.

you.

REALITY LIKES TO BEAT
OUR IMAGINATION INTO
SUBMISSION.
THAT IS THE JOB
OF REALITY.

BUT WHERE DID
THIS PARTICULAR
VERSION OF REALITY
COME FROM?
HOW DID WE LEARN
TO SUPPRESS OUR
IMAGINATION AND
BE SO DOGGEDLY
EFFICIENT
AND REALISTIC?

A C⊗G IN *a* WHEEL

Three hundred years of history has taught us a lot about thinking in straight lines. The Industrial Revolution began the transition from hand-production methods to machine manufacturing. We were pulled from the fields and our lives in the country to fill the factories and the assembly lines of the cities. In an instant our old agrarian lives were gone and our new factory life began.

REPETITION

The job was simple. Do one task in the most efficient way possible. Do it over and over again without thinking, do the same thing all day long, twelve hours a day, six days a week, and whatever you do, don't stop the line. This mechanization of workers was incredible for maximizing profits, and it became the engine that powered Europe's and then the world's economic explosion. We became human machines that were taught and expected to fulfill one task. There was no room in this equation for thought, purpose, or imagination.

"The man whose whole life is spent in performing a few simple operations, of which the effects are perhaps always the same, or very nearly the same, has no occasion to exert his understanding or to exercise his invention in finding out expedients for removing difficulties which never occur. He naturally loses, therefore, the habit of such exertion... "

ADAM SMITH *The Wealth of Nations*

What happens to a person when they are treated like a small part of a big machine and then are pushed past the point of exhaustion for days and weeks and months and years? Where does the imagination go to hide?

A FACTORY
Education

As the Industrial Revolution boomed, large-scale factories needed workers to fill an ever-growing number of jobs on the assembly line. They needed a steady supply of efficient labour that could stand up under the pressure of doing the same repetitive job for long periods of time. To fill this need, the methodology of the factories was brought into the schools. Modern learning was born. A school system was developed that could build these modern workers. It would teach children to sit still at their desks, all in a row, for eight hours a day, five days a week, preparing them for a life in the factory.

"Mass systems of public education were developed primarily to meet the needs of the Industrial Revolution and, in many ways, they mirror the principles of industrial production. They emphasize linearity, conformity and standardization. One of the reasons they are not working now is that real life is organic, adaptable and diverse."

KEN ROBINSON *Out of Our Minds*

The organizational efficiency of factories and schools has seamlessly migrated into the culture of modern business institutions. Office towers stand like endless white-collar factories. Rows and rows of cubicles and computers, stretching for miles under yellow neon lights, have become the norm. Almost every factory, school, or office around the world is now organized in this way. But this organizational efficiency isn't just about how we structurally organize ourselves; it is also reflected in the way we are programmed to think.

STRAIGHT LINE
Thinking

The shortest distance between two points is a straight line. It is the fastest and most efficient way to get from point A to point B. "As the crow flies." In a world that values cost-effective, utilitarian efficiency, straight-line thinking has become the dominant methodology. Work fast, work cheap, and deliver on time. This kind of thinking is fantastic for productivity on the assembly line and in big classrooms where "no child gets left behind," but it is the death of creativity and imagination. When we think in straight lines we negate options. We stifle possibilities because we are always concerned with the efficiency of getting to the result. We cut ourselves off from exploration, experimentation, and play, trading our broad imagination for the quick answer or the status quo result that we know will "work" and satisfy.

IT'S MUCH EASIER,
FASTER, AND
"SAFER"
TO COPY
WHAT HAS BEEN DONE
BEFORE RATHER THAN
TO STRUGGLE FOR
WHAT IS POSSIBLE.

A

FAST *and* **PREDICTABLE**

B

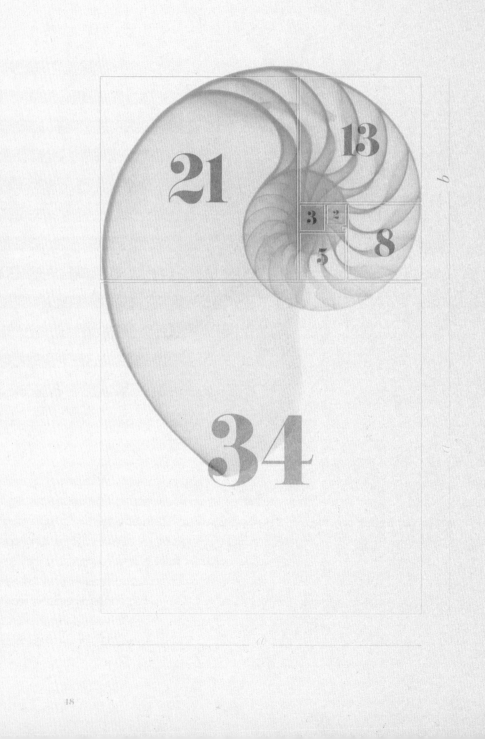

We LOVE PATTERNS

To aliens looking down at us from their high orbit it must be confusing. "How do they keep to those perfect lines and form such intricate patterns?" they must wonder. "What kind of hive mind keeps them all conforming and working together?"

If we could see ourselves at night, through a telescope from space, what would we see? First, just the earth — all the continents and oceans. Then, pushing in a little closer, the outlines of cities, sprawling into the dark. Next, the complex patterns of traffic, lights, and movement. Lastly, us, in ant-like lines, then in small groups, and, finally, alone as individuals.

For 99.9 percent of the magnification process, we would all look the same, part of the morphing geometry of the patterns and routines we follow and repeat over and over. It is only with the final turn of the knob that any of our individuality would come become visible.

Human beings are creatures of habit. We love patterns, we love predictability, and we love routine. We tend to go to the same places, to do the same things in the same ways most of the time. Trying something new is, for most of us, the exception rather than the rule. It's not surprising, really. We are constantly surrounded by patterns. Some can be seen easily with the naked eye: the growth rings of a tree, the veins in a leaf, and the designs in a butterfly's wing. Others, like the Fibonacci sequence and the golden ratio, live beneath the surface in the hidden mathematical patterns that make up nature itself. Patterns are an integral part of our lives. It is completely natural for us to want to retreat to the safety of our routines. But to be creative, we need to go against our nature and step outside these patterns. We need to look at the world from different angles. The creator's job is to observe all the varying patterns that continually surround us and then generate mutations that alter the outcome of the pattern and design.

BY ACTING ON OBSERVATIONS, WE CREATE MUTATION, AND MUTATIONS ARE THE BASIS OF CREATIVITY.

If you take the same numbers and run them through the same computation, you naturally expect the same result. Why would the equation be any different with creativity? If you or your team are not getting the creative results you want, try changing some of the elements in the computation.

START
MESSING WITH
YOUR PATTERNS

ACTION

FIVE

Practise breaking your patterns.
Start with the small things.

These are simple exercises, but when you start to break even your smallest patterns others begin to reveal themselves. So much of our lives are guided by habit and routine. When you begin to alter these patterns you have taken the first steps to reigniting your creative-thinking centre. Instead of blindly following, you are choosing alternatives. Through these tiny actions, you are physicalizing change. Making it real. When you force yourself to step outside of habit, you will begin to see your life from a new perspective.

MAKE YOUR COFFEE A **DIFFERENT** WAY. ◯

EAT AT A **NEW** LUNCH SPOT. ⬡

CHOOSE SOMETHING DIFFERENT FROM THE MENU. ⬡

TAKE AN **ALTERNATIVE** ROUTE TO WORK. ⬡

SIT NEXT TO SOMEONE NEW AT A MEETING. ◯

SLEEP ON THE **OTHER SIDE** OF THE BED. ⬡

WEAR THAT **FUNKY** PAIR OF SHOES. ◯

READ FICTION / READ NON-FICTION / READ POETRY ⬡

IF YOU NORMALLY GO TO YOGA, TRY KICK-BOXING **INSTEAD.** ◯

IF YOU DO KICK-BOXING, GO TO MEDITATION. ⬡

WE LOVE
the RULES

Just as we love to keep to our patterns, we also love to create and follow rules. Our lives are made up of a million rules, and every day we encounter rules that constrain and influence our actions and our thinking. The rules of law, the rules of work, rules of religion, culture, relationships, peer pressure, and a thousand other tiny unwritten rules that we follow without question or second thought. We are constantly guided by an invisible hand that keeps us within the boundaries.

Most of the time, we love the rules. They keep us safe. They give us dependable and predictable outcomes, and in the Real World that is exactly what we want.

If I am driving in my car and I have a green light, and you are driving in the opposite direction and you have a red light, I love knowing that when we both get to the intersection, you are going to stop.

IN THE REAL WORLD WE WANT AND NEED PREDICTABLE OUTCOMES

We need to know that certain things in our lives will operate in predictable ways. According to the rules. Without that predictability our lives, and society as a whole, descend into anarchy.

BUT CREATIVITY IS NOT THE REAL WORLD

In the world of creativity we are searching for amazing outcomes — outcomes that defy the status quo's version of reality and logic. We want outcomes that we never could have predicted at the beginning of the creative process. For creativity to work we need to embrace unpredictability. We need to

STEP OUTSIDE THE RULES

SECURITY

THE 4th WALL

In "theatre speak" there is an imaginary wall that separates the actors from the audience. It runs along the front edge of the stage, forming an invisible barrier between the two. It is called the 4th wall. In most traditional theatre productions the rule is "you don't cross the 4th wall." This wall forms the boundary of the imaginary world the actors are creating, allowing the audience to suspend their disbelief and commit fully to the story that is unfolding in front of them. From their seats, all the audience members have a clear, unobstructed view and have a very similar experience. Both parties, actors and audience, understand these rules of separation, and this provides predictability. They can all safely enjoy their ninety minutes together inside of their respective comfort zones. Everyone understands how the system works, what's generally coming next, and what their role is for the evening.

STEPPING ACROSS

Every show I play or presentation I give — whether it's for 400 or 40,000 — I always try to cross the 4th wall, and the reason is simple. When you do, it automatically changes the relationship you have with the audience and blows open the possibilities of what can happen. The second I cross the threshold of the 4th wall, the level of risk goes up. I no longer have the protection of the stage, physically or metaphorically. I lose the power of the stage's elevation, the dramatic lighting, and the myth of "distance." When I am standing in an audience singing, talking, or in an unscripted conversation, suddenly anything can happen. I have no idea how the audience will react. I am forced to follow the script as it unfolds live rather than how it was written, and suddenly none of us knows how the story will end. I have increased the chances of something or everything going disastrously wrong. But by doing so, I have also created the circumstances where incredible moments can happen. These are the moments that I never could have imagined or written in advance.

UNPREDICTABILITY
OPENS THE DOOR TO POSSIBILITY

If you never let anything unexpected happen, nothing unexpected will happen. The creative process is about discovering the answer, not knowing it in advance. If you want to have amazing creative experiences, you need to open up to risk and cross your own 4th wall. Creativity demands it.

ENCOURAGE UNEXPECTED OUTCOMES

Curved LINE THINKING

Imagining and then building something out of one's imagination is messy work. It does not follow the straight lines society has painstakingly taught us to worship. Crows don't actually fly in straight lines, and nor does the creative process. Creativity is inefficient. It meanders around corners and weaves through empty alleys. It is constantly bumping into walls and falling off ledges. While the straight line flies overhead and gets to its destination faster, creativity has to observe, study, and explore all the various points of interest along the way. The people who undertake this work know they must follow the curves where they lead. They follow their imagination and the dream in their heads, however irrational. It is in these curves that creativity happens. It is the ability to doggedly hunt down a dream until it can be satisfied in reality. The goal and the finish line are always important, but they are balanced by the need to realize the vision.

IF YOU WERE GOING TO START A BUSINESS TODAY, WHAT WOULD YOU DO?

Ten years ago the standard starting point would have been to create an intricate, highly developed plan projecting every detail of your future business. A hard-copy vision of what you would be doing, your customers, and how it would all roll out. The five-year plan.

Today things are a bit different. The rise of the start-up and start-up culture is changing the way business thinks about planning, and about the straight lines of business plans. Steve Blank, Silicon Valley serial-entrepreneur and academic, writes: "Business plans rarely survive first contact with customers. As the boxer Mike Tyson once said about his opponents' prefight strategies: 'Everybody has a plan until they get punched in the mouth.'"

These days, powered by the Internet, small teams of entrepreneurs are able to build giant businesses by utilizing the agile thinking of the modern start-up. It looks a bit like this:

1

Idea for a business

2

Build a minimal viable product (MVP),
the smallest possible version that can still viably
test the idea (minimal features).

3

Go out into the world and test the MVP with customers
to see if it works, how they react and collect feedback.

4

Based on the feedback, implement fast iterations
and push out new features quickly.

5

If it's working, and traction and
retention are growing, continue.

6

If it's not working, it's time to pivot
and radically change direction.

"If you are not embarrassed by the first version of your product, you've launched too late."

REID HOFFMAN *LinkedIn*

This new breed of entrepreneur has learned to think and react quickly, to follow the curves of the creative process where they lead rather than just march to some predetermined, arbitrary place. The destination is visualized but not written in stone. The discoveries made along the way have immense influence on the course of the journey. Some of today's most famous new companies started out doing something else. They had an idea they thought would work but changed direction midstream to focus on something completely different. They followed the path where it led.

NOTORIOUS PIVOTS

INSTAGRAM
This viral photo app, which sold to Facebook for $1 billion (said with an Austin Powers accent), started out as a location-based service called Burbn.

PAYPAL
Began as a cryptography company that exchanged money over PalmPilots.

YOUTUBE
Was a video-dating site called Tune In Hook Up.

TWITTER
Was originally Odeo, a platform for podcasting. And the list goes on…

A NEW REVOLUTION

IS CREATIVE THINKING
AN INVESTMENT OR AN EXPENSE?

In a world where a company's business model can stay the same year after year, where you can count on stability within your discipline or industry, where you know that your job will still exist five years from now and it is very possible that you will be employed by the same company for most of your life, it is easy to consider time spent on creative thinking as an expense. Everything is stable. Just keep doing what you are doing because it's all running smoothly. Why invest in new ideas when everything is golden? What could possibly go wrong?

AND THEN ALONG CAME THE INTERNET
AND CHANGED EVERYTHING...

I was signed to EMI Records in Canada for ten years and in my time there I watched them go from almost four hundred employees down to around thirty. It was a slow, painful descent that finally ended when EMI was taken over by Universal in

September 2012. Through the years I kept thinking, why don't they do something? Why can't they innovate themselves out of this mess? They have the resources, they own the product, and they have this immense infrastructure.

In retrospect, given the kind of company EMI was and the corporate culture they had, winning the war in the new digital environment would have been almost impossible. EMI had been doing the same thing since it was established in London in 1897. They found artists, recorded their music, pressed that music onto vinyl or plastic, and then distributed, marketed, and sold those flat discs to the world. By 1997 they had built up an intricate worldwide distribution system and large physical manufacturing plants to make their compact discs, all controlled by a traditional hierarchical management structure. Their business was based on a model of scarcity. Music imprinted on physical discs had value because there were a limited number of them. No shiny disc, no music. Once music could be digitized, compressed, and transferred anywhere in the world in seconds, that scarcity disappeared. In the age of the Internet and the age of digital, 90 percent of the infrastructure EMI had spent a hundred years building became irrelevant almost overnight. They were a company that had been doing the same thing over and over again, very successfully, for a century. They had no real need for radical creative thinking within their company because their business model had stayed pretty much the same. When digital hit, they suddenly needed to come up with radical innovative solutions and rapidly change.

Traditional big businesses are like giant cruise ships. They turn very slowly and they have to plan those turns well in advance so they don't crash into the shore. Expecting EMI to be able to adapt quickly enough to the changes that were happening almost overnight is kind of like expecting crocodiles to climb trees. It was impossible because it simply wasn't part of their nature. In the Internet age, where everything is moving so much faster, you need to weave innovation and creativity into your company culture. This is a long-term project. Creativity is something you have to learn and slowly breed into your DNA. You can't slap it on at the end as an afterthought when you suddenly realize you need it.

"Nothing is so painful to the human mind as a great and sudden change."

MARY SHELLEY *Frankenstein*

IN THIS NEW
FAST-MOVING,
EVER-CHANGING
ENVIRONMENT,
CREATIVITY IS
NOT A LUXURY
OR A RISK.
IT REALLY IS
A NECESSITY.

ACTION

◇◇◇◇◇◇◇◇◇◇◇◇◇◇◇◇◇◇◇◇◇◇◇◇◇◇◇◇◇◇◇◇◇◇◇

SIX

Do you consider time spent on creative thinking
an **INVESTMENT** or an **EXPENSE**?

⬡   ⬡

How has your industry or genre been
affected by the Internet Revolution?

What are the specific changes you have
witnessed over the last five years?

What changes do you see on the horizon?

INVESTING IN *the* CURVE

Opening up your imagination to new ideas doesn't just happen by chance or by luck. It takes work and commitment. It takes investment. To some, the idea that we need to invest in our imagination might seem peculiar at best. It's an odd concept, investing in the imagination.

WHO HAS THE TIME OR MONEY TO SPEND IT WANDERING THE CURVES OF CREATIVITY?

It turns out that many of today's most innovative and creative companies do, and they have actively moved their companies to invest in creativity and the imagination of "the curve."

At Google, 20 percent of an employee's time can be spent working on personal projects that interest them. These are exploratory projects born from an individual employee's imagination and curiosity. Gmail, Google News, Google Talk, and

AdSense all began as personal employees' side projects and were developed on company time. In a talk at Stanford University, Marissa Mayer, Google's vice-president of search products and user experience until July 2012, revealed that half of all new product launches at the time had originated from the Innovation Time Off entrepreneurship program. Apple followed suit and in 2012 launched their own more limited Blue Sky program, which allows selected employees to take two weeks a year to work on personal projects outside their normal responsibilities.

But this isn't a new idea. Since 1948, 3M has encouraged its employees to spend 15 percent of their time working on their own projects. 3M is one of the most innovative companies in the world, making over 55,000 different products and launching more than a thousand new ones each year.

While Google, Apple, and 3M are all massive companies, the idea of allotting time for creativity is not just for big corporations. This is an idea that works on any scale. It's not rocket science. If you want to be more creative, you need to invest time in the process of creativity. If you want to find innovative solutions, you need to spend time innovating. It is the same process, whether you are a global company, a small business, or just a person.

> **"There is no way that this winter is ever going to end as long as this groundhog keeps seeing his shadow. I don't see any other way out. He's got to be stopped. And I have to stop him."**
>
> PHIL CONNORS *Groundhog Day*

THE *Half-*HOUR HABIT

My friend Shelly is a writer. She writes about travel and fitness for a number of small magazines and web sites. Shelly gets up every day at 6 a.m., puts on the coffee, takes half an hour to dig into her email and check the news, and then launches into her writing. Every day rolls out pretty much the same way, divided between writing, researching, interviewing, talking to editors, bookkeeping, and invoicing. By the time the day is done and she closes up her computer around 6 p.m., Shelly is spent and exhausted. Every couple of months we get together for a drink and inevitably the conversation turns to her work. "It's burning me out," she says. "I am stuck on a technical-writing treadmill that I can't get off, and it never stops!" I empathize, and each time my advice is the same: "Shelly, maybe as an experiment, try taking the first half hour of every day — before the emails, before reading the news, before scrolling through Facebook, before you start working — and spend that time on ideas. Use that time to generate ideas to grow and change your business, on creative ways of getting off the treadmill. Invest that time in yourself." Her reply is always the same:

"I'd love to but I can't. I've got way too much to do."

It is not easy to adhere to the half-hour habit. Distractions are everywhere. Work is calling and the emails are piling up. Sitting there thinking and exploring can feel like time wasted, but if you want different results you need to implement a different process. The half-hour habit is a great place to start.

My half hour happens first thing in the morning, starting at 5 a.m. before the kids wake up and the noise of the day throws my brain into chaos. (Over time, my half hour has expanded to an hour and a half.) Sometimes I spend it reading and following my curiosity; sometimes it's spent developing a specific project. This is the time of day that works for me and it's something I have been doing religiously for the past twenty years. Developing a routine and a ritual is the key to keeping your creativity alive. Some people will be most creative late at night, some in the afternoon. It is crucial to discover the time of day and the circumstances when you feel the most connected to your creative self, and then to consistently carve out that time for creative thinking.

**"See,
I observed Escher,
I love Basquiat
I watched Keith Haring,
you see I studied art
The greats weren't great
because at birth they could paint
The greats were great
cause they paint a lot"**

MACKLEMORE & RYAN LEWIS *Ten Thousand Hours*

EVERY *Day*

In 2010 I went to see Malcolm Gladwell speak in Montreal, where he described a few stories from his book *Outliers*. He talked about Mozart, who has long been considered a boy genius, and how he had actually apprenticed and studied for many years. Mozart started very young, and his music-teacher father was a driving force in his son's development, work ethic, and career. Gladwell went on to talk about the Beatles and Fleetwood Mac and how in each of these cases talent had been a factor but the real key to success was 10,000 hours of practice and dedication.

As he finished his talk and I got up to leave, I couldn't help but feel slightly underwhelmed. Malcolm Gladwell is an amazing, charismatic speaker and I am a huge fan of all his previous books, but for some reason I didn't really get it. Outside in the hallway I could hear others around me raving about his talk, but I was just confused. Later, I went over his examples with my artist friends, outlining them point by point. They all had the same reaction: "Huh? So what?"

To working artists the concept of "10,000 hours" of dedication seems so obvious it doesn't need to be said. Ten thousand hours is a given. Artists know from experience that what appears, at first glance, to be divinely anointed talent is really countless hours of study and endless drive. Talent matters, but work is what delivers you. This notion is counterintuitive to the popular mythology propagated about the artist. Artists get up late, do their art for a bit, and then the rest of the day is spent reading Bukowski, drinking red wine, and then it's on to lots and lots of free love. (There is some of that.) Working artists know that to get really good at their creative discipline, they have to work incredibly hard. You have to put in the time and invest in your craft.

**CREATIVITY IS AN INVESTMENT
AND LIKE ANY INVESTMENT THERE ARE
RISKS AND THERE ARE NO GUARANTEES.
THE ONLY TRUE GUARANTEE IS THAT
IF YOU DON'T INVEST IN YOUR IMAGINATION,
YOU WILL NOT BECOME MORE CREATIVE.**

IF YOU THINK
YOU ARE NOT
VERY CREATIVE,
ASK YOURSELF
HOW MUCH TIME
YOU HAVE
ACTUALLY DEVOTED
TO THE PURSUIT
OF CREATIVITY.

ACTION

SEVEN

Start the half-hour habit.

Experiment with your schedule to find out how you can realistically introduce this creative half hour into your day. Find out what times work best for you. To change any patterned behaviour and start new habits we need to be dogmatic and a bit relentless with methodology. Be disciplined about writing down the days you do your creative half hour and the days you miss. Note the time of day of each session and then do a quick rating of the session from **1** to **10**.

1 = *This time of day sucks and I wish I was in bed.*
10 = *I'm a fucking creative genius.*

Figure out when you are the most open, engaged, and productive with your creative half hour. And then stick to it.

Every day starting now…

DAY 1

TIME OF THE DAY

RATING

1 2 3 4 5 6 7 8 9 10

DAY 2

TIME OF THE DAY

RATING

1 2 3 4 5 6 7 8 9 10

DAY 3

TIME OF THE DAY

RATING

1 2 3 4 5 6 7 8 9 10

TIME OF

RATING

1 2 3

DAY 4

TIME OF THE DAY

RATING

1 2 3 4 5 6 7 8 9 10

DAY 5

TIME OF THE DAY

RATING

1 2 3 4 5 6 7 8 9 10

DAY 6

TIME OF THE DAY

RATING

1 2 3 4 5 6 7 8 9 10

TIME OF

RATING

1 2 3

DAY 7

TIME OF THE DAY

RATING

1 2 3 4 5 6 7 8 9 10

DAY 8

TIME OF THE DAY

RATING

1 2 3 4 5 6 7 8 9 10

DAY 9

TIME OF THE DAY

RATING

1 2 3 4 5 6 7 8 9 10

TIME OF

RATING

1 2 3

DAY 10

TIME OF THE DAY

RATING

1 2 3 4 5 6 7 8 9 10

DAY 11

TIME OF THE DAY

RATING

1 2 3 4 5 6 7 8 9 10

DAY 12

TIME OF THE DAY

RATING

1 2 3 4 5 6 7 8 9 10

TIME OF

RATING

1 2 3

THE EXCUSE *of* TIME AND SPACE

ARE YOU WAITING FOR PERFECTION?

We all have an image in our mind's eye of the perfect time and space to do our creative work. An amazing studio overlooking the ocean with the brilliant light of a sunset washing colour through the floor-to-ceiling windows. Eight uninterrupted hours in which we can really focus and let our minds wander around a problem. Being surrounded by like-minded people who inspire and drive us. A supportive community. The perfect co-founder — experienced, inspiring, and connected. It all sounds so good. And then a screaming four-year-old runs through the picture and it all comes crashing back down to earth.

The reality of the creative life is that there is never enough time and space, and conditions are never perfect. Our lives are always full of a never-ending list of things to do that fill our time and separate us from the work we know we should be doing.

TWEET
TWEET

The mind is a funny thing. It convinces us that we want, more than anything in the world, to just dive into our creative process and get down to work. At the same time, it allows us to stray and fall victim to every distraction. In today's modern world of pings and tweets, DMs and texts, the temptations are everywhere. We are living in a distraction economy, with everyone vying for the same attention for their 140 characters. The world will surely stop if an @yournamehere does not get an instant reply. Now more than ever, to do work and to be creative in this environment we need to be vigilant. We have to find, and fight, for time and mental space amid the chaos.

Conditions will never be perfect. So just start.

"THE EXCUSE OF TIME AND SPACE"
was first printed in the Huffington Post *as*
"The Perfect Time to Get Creative Is Now."
*It marked the moment when I really started to imagine
that just maybe I could write this book.*

Dream
ELEPHANTS

CRAZY UNCLE HARRY

The line between being Crazy Uncle Harry in the tinfoil hat muttering on about another wacky idea and the genius renaissance visionary who can "see the future" is very thin indeed.

YOU HAVE TO RISK A LITTLE CRAZY IF YOU EVER HOPE TO ESCAPE THE GRAVITATIONAL PULL OF THE ORDINARY

. . .

LET *the* ELEPHANT OUT OF THE B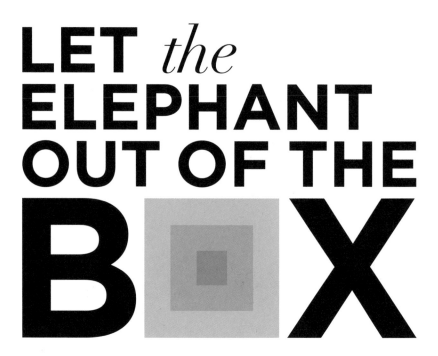X

I am lucky enough to be surrounded by an incredible group of friends. Some are geek entrepreneurs but most are experimental artists and modern dancers. These are people who live for their art and are the definition of Icarus. They fly high, burn very hot and very bright. They have heightened emotions and they live fully but there is no big payout waiting at the end. No pot of gold. The one thing these artists understand is the passion of creativity, the burning desire to do something even though it goes against all logic. All financial logic. All physical logic. Against all the laws of common sense, and definitely outside the scope of the status quo. These people know how to access their crazy limitless imaginations. These friends teach me every day — about reaching beyond perceived limits, and about how to dream outside the borders of the realistic world.

"I've never been certain whether the moral of the Icarus story should only be, as is generally accepted, 'don't try to fly too high,' or whether it might also be thought of as 'forget the wax and feathers, and do a better job on the wings.'"

STANLEY KUBRICK

Pushing hard on the boundaries and being "experimental" may not be where you need your imagination to live full-time for your creativity to function, but there is great value in being able to visit this place once in a while. The ability to vacation our imagination on the edge gives us the ability to expand our mind, opening us up to a whole new world of possibility.

Next page, some friends in
LE NOMBRE D'OR *(Live)* ▸
COMPAGNIE MARIE CHOUINARD

ACTION

EIGHT

To get your imagination in motion you need to expose yourself to different ideas, people, and places. It's time to leave the nest. If you want a dynamic imagination, you need to infuse it with dynamic ideas. Take your brain out for a walk. Get out of the house and experience something new. A dance show, a lecture at the local university, a band that you would never normally see, a conference outside of your discipline — anything outside of your ordinary that might create a spark. Start to open yourself to ideas that live beyond your comfort zone. Be dogmatic. For each of the next four weeks choose something different that takes your mind somewhere it would not normally wander. Think: open, experimental, experiential.

_____

WEEK 1

WEEK 2

WEEK 3

WEEK 4

PINK ELEPHANTS & PURPLE COWS

In Seth Godin's now-classic book *Purple Cow*, he uses the term to describe building something remarkable and unique that will stand out in a world of normal. "Something worth talking about. Worth noticing. Exceptional. New. Interesting. It's a Purple Cow. Boring stuff is invisible. It's a brown cow." In a world where we are constantly inundated by ever-increasing piles of "stuff," it has become increasingly important to be different and to produce things that have remarkable qualities. The Internet gives everyone the same opportunity to broadcast their creative work, both good and bad. Your ability to be remarkable is what separates you from the herd and allows you to rise above the endless sea of creativity that flows past every day. In order to build a Purple Cow product you need a great idea.

YOU NEED PINK ELEPHANT THINKING.

"Had a dream
I could turn back time
Had to stop
to rewind my memory
Had a vision of the ruby sky
We were riding high on
our own pink elephant"

DAVID USHER *from the song* "HOW ARE YOU?"

In my creative circle, during brainstorming sessions, we have always called big, ridiculous, unlikely ideas Pink Elephants. These Pink Elephant ideas are rare, they are shy, and they can retreat into the fog in an instant. These are the crazy ideas that come from big dreams and a wide imagination. They often seem impossible and not grounded in reality, so it is always tempting to immediately dismiss them and to send them back into the wild without a second thought.

"That is totally bananas. It will never work. No, no, no!"

Our natural instinct and all of our training will push us toward the logical, realistic ideas that seem "doable." It is far too easy to limit ourselves and others. It's much harder to allow your imagination to play unbound by the confines of common sense. Exploring Pink Elephant ideas can lead you to places you never could have reached by limiting yourself to the "realistic." There will be plenty of time later in the creative process for reality to beat an idea down to size. Start by letting your imagination run wild. Let the Pink Elephants loose and see where they lead.

Listen to the song **"HOW ARE YOU?"** *at* lettheelephantsrun.com

IF YOU STRIVE TO DREAM
WILD PINK ELEPHANTS,
BY THE TIME YOUR IDEA
HAS BEEN REALIZED
YOU WILL BE LUCKY
TO GET AN ELEPHANT.

IF YOU DREAM
ELEPHANTS,
YOU MAY END UP
WITH A DONKEY.

IF YOUR DREAM
IS DONKEY-SIZED,
YOU WILL BE LUCKY
BY THE END OF YOUR
PROCESS TO END UP
WITH THE DRAWING OF
A SMALL WET DOG.

PINK ELEPHANT IDEA:
Heartbeat

Every time the band takes the stage we set the rhythm and become the heartbeat of the evening. We set the tone and timbre. We determine how the audience moves and, if we are doing our jobs, how they feel. I started to question this dynamic and began to wonder how I could reverse-engineer this idea. How could I get the audience to power the band? Over time I distilled the idea further: How could I choose one audience member and have the band play to their heartbeat?

Now, you might rightly ask, "Why would anyone want to do that?" The simple answer is,

I wanted to see what would happen.

I believed there was something interesting in the experiment. I had that feeling, an itch to scratch, but at the time I was busy on tour so I filed the idea away.

A year later, in July 2011, I was surfing through Kickstarter looking at different crowdfunding campaigns when I came across the Pulse Sensor Open Source Heart-Rate Sensor. The founders were looking to make a small heart-rate sensor that could be customized using an Arduino circuit board. I immediately paid my $38 and waited to see if the project would get funded. Six months later, my Pulse Sensor arrived and I began hunting for someone in Montreal that knew how to build and program Arduino. After some searching I found Rupert Brooks, who runs Foulab, a Montreal hacker space. I explained my crazy idea to him and he immediately jumped on board. The reason was simple:

He wanted to see what would happen.

After a few months of experimenting, trying out three different kinds of heart-rate monitors, and Rupert writing a customized algorithm that could smooth out weird irregularities of the human heartbeat, we finally had a working prototype. I started using the heart-rate monitor during special concerts and at conferences during my presentations on creativity and the creative process.

THE EXPERIMENT

During my presentations I pull a nervous volunteer out of the audience, hook them up to the monitor, and suddenly the loud pounding of their heartbeat fills the room. Jonathan (my friend and guitarist) starts to play and then I begin to sing. We improvise live to the rhythm of the volunteer's beating heart. I use this demonstration as an example of experimentation, risk, and creativity. It has become the climax of my presentations, and each time gets a huge reaction from the audience:

Because: they want to see what happens.

When I first had the Pink Elephant idea, there was no thought about where it would lead, how I would use it, or if it had "value." It was simply an experiment I felt I had to try.

SOMETIMES
YOU LEAD THE
IDEAS
AND SOMETIMES
THE IDEAS LEAD YOU.
THEY ALWAYS
TAKE YOU PLACES
YOU DIDN'T EXPECT.

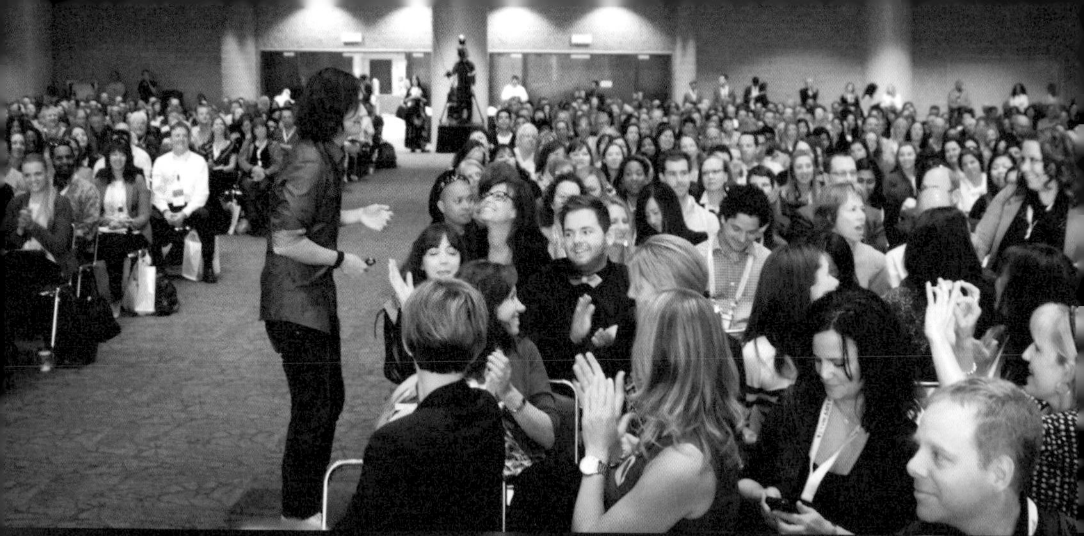

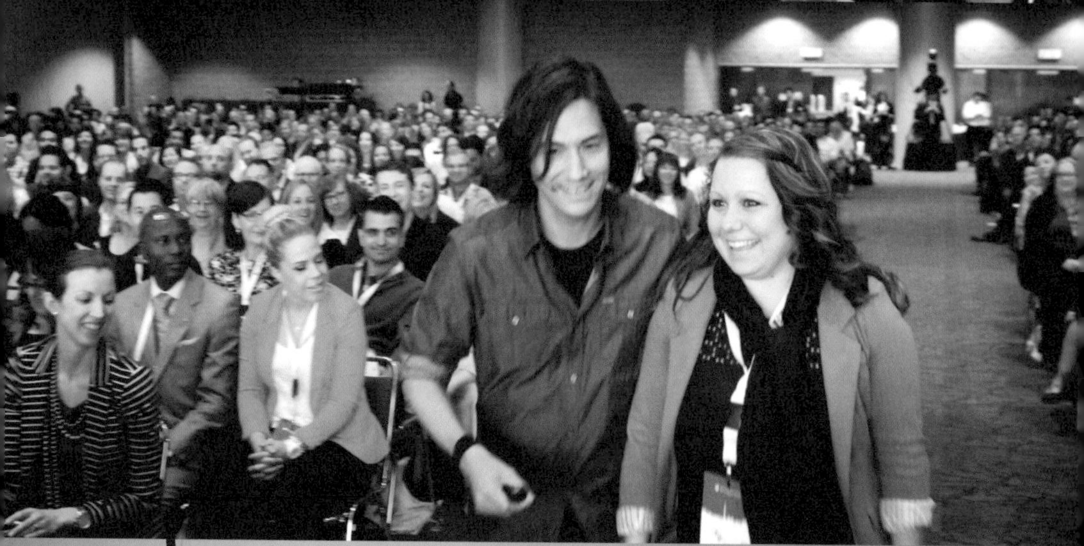

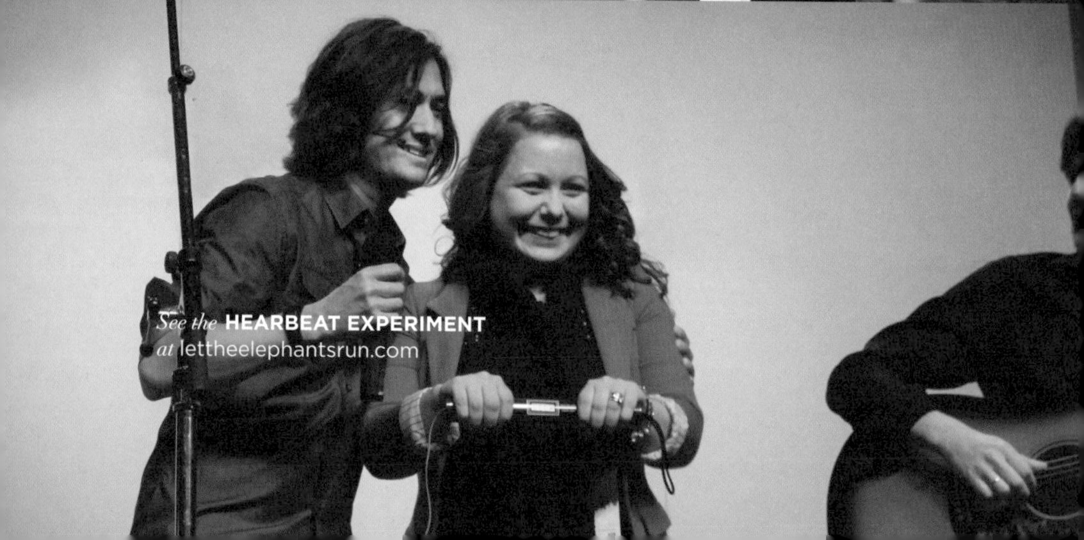

See the **HEARBEAT EXPERIMENT**
at lettheelephantsrun.com

ACTION

NINE

Think about your own Pink Elephants.
I know you've had them. Ideas that seemed
too big, unwieldy, and unrealistic.

Write down a few of your own Pink Elephant ideas.

Dark
PASSENGERS:
RESISTANCE *&* FEAR

**It creeps in quietly,
that voice in my head,
the small doubt that grows
throughout the night.
It is a constant and I beat
it back daily for fear
it will take me over.**

The danger is always there. To be taken over and swept away by the big roadblocks of creative process which are resistance and fear. You must be vigilant to monitor and control these two dark passengers because they are the killers of creativity.

The INTERNAL VOICE

It is our nature to want to minimize risk and neutralize pain. If you accidentally touch your hand to a hot burner, it is the nerve endings — that ancient wiring — that shocks the brain into jerking your hand away. Creativity is both risky and emotionally painful, and our instincts will implore us to retreat to safer ground. As we begin to take risks, pushing the limits of our boundaries, and as we attempt to build something outside of our tribe, that little voice of doubt will start to grow. It will whisper all manner of unsavoury things about failure and embarrassment in order to bring us back to "safety."

The creator's job is to protect the creation at all costs, and to do that we must be victorious over resistance and fear. You will hear the nagging voice of doubt at every stage of the process. You must fight against your nature and push yourself through.

THE FRIENDS &
FAMILY FACTOR

You are so excited about your new idea and your new creative direction that you are just bursting. You want to tell the world about it so they will be just as excited. Then you can run off to the bar together and celebrate the joys and wonder of your new project and toast to your future success.

Let me tell you what happens next.

While I am sure your friends and family are wonderful people, the nature of the pack is to draw the straying beast back to the herd. They may be well intentioned, and worried that your new idea or direction doesn't sound "safe," like your old job or your old paintings or your old music. Their own resistance and fear will start to bubble to the surface as they worry how you stepping out will change the dynamic of their lives, too. This reaction does not usually come from a place of malice, but their doubts will fan the fires of your doubts and start building up an impossible mountain before you have even taken a first step.

Getting a new creative project in motion is hard enough without the doubt of others stacked against you. Do yourself a favour and keep your mouth shut. When your ideas are still newborn, treat them as something precious that needs time to grow and develop and change. There will be plenty of time to talk and discuss and defend your ideas later. Plenty of time.

Are YOU A MONSTER?

Monster / mon·ster / *noun* **1.** any creature so ugly or monstrous as to frighten people.

When you are in a creative process, collaborating with a group or listening to someone's new ideas, do you always want to be the first to give feedback? While they are talking or demonstrating something, are you leaning like a sprinter at the starting line just dying to let loose with your contrarian opinion?

Then you are probably a Monster. It's a term that can also be used as a verb. "Hey man, quit monstering me!," meaning you are not listening and allowing ideas the chance to be heard. You are injecting "No" into the creative process and creating an atmosphere that doesn't allow people to express their ideas freely without fear of getting crushed. You are killing imagination and hunting the Pink Elephants down before they can even enter the room.

BANG, BANG, CLICK, BANG!

This is a silly party game best played with friends over a few stiff drinks. The game is simple. Gather the players in a circle. You hold up your finger and thumb like you have a pistol and then you randomly point it at different people in the circle, saying:

"Bang, Bang, Click, Bang!"

Point randomly at a different person on every word. Then ask the group the question:

"Who's dead?"

Now wait a few moments. Give people time to start guessing how the game is played and why the dead person is dead. Allow enough time so people forget who spoke first. Next, point at the person who spoke first and say,

"You're dead."

Repeat the whole process until they discover the pattern. It often can take quite a long time for people to figure it out.

When my friend Stephen O'Connell introduced me to the game, we played for around ten minutes, round after round, and I was always dead. Each time I thought I had figured it out and each time I managed to jump in first with my opinion.

EUREKA

I discovered something very interesting about myself that night. I really liked to speak first. And I was spending very little time listening. I was shocked to discover...

I was a Monster.

My Type A personality — foot on the starting line, always ready to throw in my two cents, and be right — was preventing me from listening. I was missing the subtext of what was happening around me. Instead, I was focused on my own ideas and what I had to say. I have since spent a lot of time focused on learning how to listen and how to hear.

LESSON LEARNED.

The best ideas don't always come from the loudest places and the biggest voices. Just because you can shout louder and before anyone else doesn't make your ideas better or your imagination broader. There is great value in listening and giving ideas a chance to exist and germinate. It is in the nature of the extrovert to talk and suck up all the oxygen in the room. Instead, try holding your breath for a minute and listening. This is something I still struggle with, but I'm getting a little better. Ideas can come from all kinds of places. Give everyone's Pink Elephants a little room to run.

Are YOU A MOUSE?

In Susan Cain's book *Quiet: The Power of Introverts in a World That Can't Stop Talking*, she outlines the strength and power that come from listening. Introverts are people who need a different set of circumstances to be comfortable, productive, and successful in the world of extroversion that surrounds them.

She describes introverts as people who "may have strong social skills and enjoy parties and business meetings, but after a while wish they were home in their pyjamas. They prefer to devote their social energies to close friends, colleagues, and family. They listen more than they talk, think before they speak, and often feel as if they express themselves better in writing than in conversation. They tend to dislike conflict. Many have a horror of small talk, but enjoy deep discussions."

The power to listen gives introverts a distinct competitive advantage in many creative disciplines. They intuitively know how to listen and observe, and this gives them the ability to see and collect ideas from the world around them more readily. It is easier to see more when you are not focused on being the life of the party. Cain goes on to say, "Don't think of introversion as something that needs to be cured... stay true to your own nature. If you like to do things in a slow and steady way, don't let others make you feel as if you have to race. If you enjoy depth, don't force yourself to seek breadth. If you prefer single-tasking to multi-tasking, stick to your guns. Being relatively unmoved by rewards gives you the incalculable power to go your own way."

Introversion can provide incredible creative power given the right set of circumstances. Unfortunately, the flip side of this is that when the conditions are less than perfect, for some people, introversion can quickly turn and become painful, heart-stopping shyness.

AN INTROVERT CAN QUICKLY TRANSFORM INTO A 🐁. THERE IS A DIFFERENCE.

Where the introvert is empowered by their quiet nature, the 🐁 is someone who is frozen by it, whose introversion has paralyzed their creativity and prevents them from fulfilling their creative potential. Creativity does not respect one's desire for perfect conditions. It doesn't care what you need. It will throw a wrench into your process and mess everything up.

In this modern world of fast-flowing ideas, just as the Monster needs to learn to listen, sometimes the 🐁 needs to shout. Even disciplines once considered "quiet professions" are now getting louder. The demands of creativity do not always allow Mice or even introverts to move at their chosen pace or within the narrowly defined parameters of their comfort zone.

THE WRITER

The artistic dream of the writer, solitary and alone, pushing out the pages and then mailing in the final manuscript. Do you still think you can be an author and just write from your country cottage and let your publisher and agent do all the rest? Wrong. These days, publishers demand that you get out there and sell your book. It's all about your platform. "How well are you engaging with your blog, Twitter, and Facebook followers?" "Here's your press schedule." "Get out there, sign books, and kiss babies."

It is very possible in this hyper-competitive world that you won't even have a publisher, and will decide to self-publish instead. Now you are an author, a publisher, a publicist, and an entrepreneur. At some point you are going to have to shout.

Sometimes creativity demands that the fight against its nature and win. It is important to learn how to live in a world of Monsters — not to become one, but just to get your message out.

"The quieter you become, the more you can hear."

YASUTANI ROSHI

ACTION

TEN

MONSTER or MOUSE?
Mark where you live on the scale.

MOUSE /// **MONSTER**

Become an observer of group dynamics. Ideas don't live in a vacuum. They are brought to life and championed by individuals. Start to analyze how ideas either bloom or are killed by the people around them, around you. How is your circle affecting the quality of the ideas that live or die?

*The next time you are in a social
setting, initiate a game of*

*Find out who are the MONSTERS
and who are the MICE.*

Dominant POSITIONS

More than 6 million people have watched Amy Cuddy's TED Talk "Your Body Language Shapes Who You Are." In it she describes how the ancient language of body position within animals and people not only changes perception but chemistry as well. The wide arms of the gorilla before it beats its chest and the victory pose of the sprinter, arms stretched out as she thrusts across the finish line, are both power poses we all intuitively understand. These non-verbal visual cues imply dominance and can change how others perceive us. "Our bodies change our minds, and our minds can change our behaviour, and our behaviour can change our outcomes." According to Cuddy, holding power poses for as little as two minutes not only changes how others perceive you but also alters your brain chemistry. Standing in postures of confidence can increase your levels of testosterone (the risk-taking, confidence hormone) and decrease your levels of cortisol (the stress hormone). You not only look more confident to others, your brain chemistry actually makes you more confident.

DOES IT WORK?

I could wake up from a dead sleep, walk out of my bus directly onto a festival stage, and play music in front of 40,000 people without skipping a beat. No nerves, no panic. I've played thousands of shows and just know how to do it. I have always felt incredibly comfortable as long as I had the "script" of the songs to support me. Public speaking is a different story. I have always been nervous speaking in front of large groups of people. A small group was fine, but something about large groups freaked me out. Even when I was little, I was always that kid at the back of the class sinking into my desk, desperate not to be picked to answer the question. When I was forced to do a presentation, for a week before I would feel the anxiety and fear welling up inside me. As I presented, forcing out the words, my hands would start to shake and the papers I was holding would rattle, only amplifying the terror I was feeling.

So I find it funny that, these days, I spend a large part of my time speaking at conferences all over the world. Experience has bred confidence; I'm now much more relaxed and enjoy my job as a speaker. But even with all my experience, I sometimes still feel those old nerves welling up inside me and part of me is transported back to being that ten-year-old kid at the back of the class.

If you happen to find yourself backstage at a conference right before I go on to speak, chances are you will see Jon and me with our arms stretched wide, holding Amy Cuddy's power positions. For two minutes at a time we try various positions, experimenting to see how they affect our performance.

Does this body position really change the testosterone and cortisol levels running through us? Are our hormones telling our brains to be more confident? I honestly don't know. What I do know is that running around backstage like a sprinter crossing the finish line lightens the mood, makes us laugh, and puts us in a better frame of mind before we step onstage.

With JONATHAN GALLIVAN

ACTION

ELEVEN

Are you nervous? The next time you have to do something in front of a group of people — at a lunch, a meeting, or a presentation — try stopping into the bathroom first and holding the power pose shown. Record the results below. Start to experiment on yourself and be sure to document your progress.

*Hold this position
for two minutes or more.*

STRUC

cture

WELCOME TO *the* EMERALD CITY

As an artist I never wanted to examine what I did too closely. I felt that being overly analytical with my process was somehow unethical or unartistic. I had internalized the idea that breaking it down to its structure and "formula" would mess with my magic mojo.

It was only when I started to work on building tech for the Web and exploring start-up culture that I really began to look seriously at my own process. I started to see the incredible similarities between the ebb and flow of the creative process of building technology and the process I used to make music, albums, and videos. All the steps seemed to line up. I began to re-examine the process I was using to make music, stripping away all the extraneous artist baggage that I had built up over the years. When I laid it all out plainly, I found that I really do work with a specific formula. In every process, I repeat the same steps over and over to get to the result and the final product. I had previously never been able, or willing, to really study what I was doing and had always just done it all by instinct. Once I dove in and started to deconstruct my process, it became obvious that there really is a methodology to the madness.

Be warned: once you pull back the curtain and see the nuts and bolts of how it all works — Oz back there pulling on the levers — you can never go back. When you rip away the myth of the process you lose a certain naïveté, but what you gain in return is far greater. You get to look at the creative process as something that you can learn, something you can get better at and continually improve upon. It becomes something you can do over and over again, and eventually master. Instead of it being just a lucky mystery, it is actually a discipline that you can study. This is something the geek in me loves.

"Pay no attention to that man behind the curtain."

The Wizard of Oz

A METHODOLOGY TO *the* MADNESS

No creative person wants to believe that they are following a formula, that what they do is by the numbers. But for the creative process to work day in and day out, over weeks and months and years, there must be a structure supporting "the freedom." The artist in me loves the chaos of imagination precisely because it is wild and unruly and satisfies my vision of what it means to be an artist. But chaos without limits also denies the second half of the creative process: the ability to actually finish and deliver work. Not once, but over and over again. The structural part of the creative process is what transforms you from a one-hit wonder or a hobbyist, or just someone who got lucky, into a working creative. Chaos hates the difficult part of the process: the work and the discipline; the thoughtful, measured calculating; the endless tedium of left-brain organizing; the structured operational part of creativity.

Creativity needs both parts to work — the freedom of imagination and the structure to hang it on. Without the structure nothing works.

THERE IS NO SINGLE
STRUCTURE THAT WORKS
FOR EVERYONE.
BUT FOR EVERYONE
THERE IS A STRUCTURE
THAT WORKS.

THIS IS
SCIENCE
and YOU ARE
A SCIENTIST

I was getting ready to give my very first presentation on creativity and the creative process. The conference was booked and I was knee-deep in it, trying to design something interesting, fun, and, well, creative. During that week my father was visiting us in Montreal. Now, my dad is an incredibly intelligent person. He is a professor of microeconomics at Queen's University and he's written nine books with titles like *The Economic Prerequisite to Democracy*. He is a seasoned teacher and lecturer, so I thought he would be a perfect person to give me feedback on what I was developing. I showed him some of my first few ideas and he said:

"Now, David, I think it's very important that
you tell the people at the beginning of your talk
that while you've made some songs,
you're not a scientist."

This totally threw me and I spent the rest of the day panicking, thinking "Oh my god, I am not a scientist! What qualifies me to speak about creativity?" I woke up the next morning with two realizations.

F I R S T
Don't show people your work before you have spent enough
time with it that you can withstand a little commentary.

A N D   S E C O N D
I am a goddamn scientist.

I have a formula to my creative process. It is not random. It is very specific. Now, some people react incredibly badly to the idea of a "creative formula," so for them I'll call it "the collection of things I need, and the series of steps that form the building blocks for a successful creative adventure."

What follows is my formula. It's not always exactly the same. There are many subtle variations and it is always evolving, but it pretty much rolls out like this:

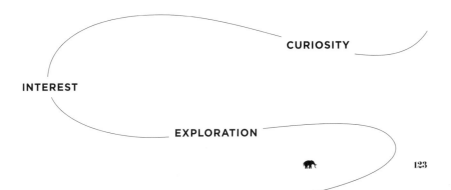

CURIOSITY

INTEREST

EXPLORATION

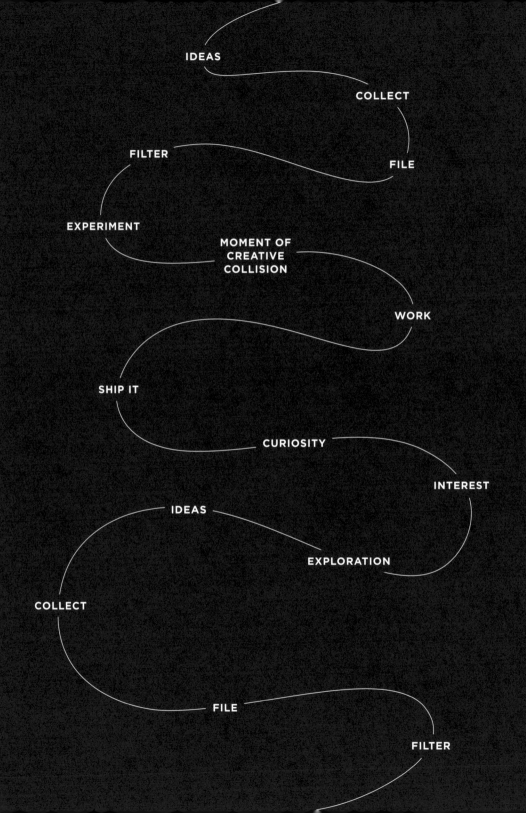

A RIVER *of* IDEAS

THE BLANK PAGE

It's sitting there, empty, staring up at me. The blank page, the empty stage, the endless white screen with the flashing cursor. "I got nothing."

STARTING SEEMS HARD,
BUT IT DOESN'T HAVE TO BE.

The easiest way to overcome the daunting blankness at the beginning of a project is to just start filling up space. Don't think. Just start working. Generate material. It doesn't have to be good, because at the beginning all you want is bulk. You are the Costco of creativity. Forget about quality. You need to fill the aisles with stuff.

Most of what you produce will end up in the trash but that doesn't matter. What you are trying to do is generate momentum, to put yourself and your process in motion.

the devision between the
creative and the contrived /
in this life of peers.
in this life of peers
we wander / like

and we are winning
a war we can't see.
the pride of predjudice
runs so deeply
and thickly and flows
loops with
acoustics.
and rage and desolate

distortions of the life
we live now
of the life we live now.
distortions of the place we
are in
I am appened up
I am opened!
who will I be when
that moment comes.
when the moment comes.
to duck at just the
right moment
and your life stays in
tact

the screaming of the crowd.
shook my emotions loose.
cracked the case
cracked the casings loose.
loose.
somewhere in this book
is a key
a key
a clue
a medical reason
a medical revival.
a merciful revision
a - revision of oneself.
the self that lives in
a thin skin
a skin coat of
soft to the touch
afl.

where has lust gone.
in the notes and the
string.
the ringg is killing me.
raw and raw
is the new foundation
clean - unclean.
out spoken and friendable.

ACTION

TWELVE

The scariest part of the blank page is
the endless blankness. Just start writing.

Fill in the page below

*Writing is one of the simplest ways to get
your ideas and imagination flowing.
Move beyond the space provided here and try filling
up one blank page in your own notebook every day.*

MAKING

To ignite our creativity we need ideas, lots and lots of ideas. But as we go through life, we naturally start to gain experience and expertise. We get good at our jobs and our careers and we get very focused. While this sounds great, it can also be the very thing that stunts our creative growth. We develop a form of adult-onset tunnel vision. As we get more focused and specialized, our childlike peripheral vision starts to blur and we stop looking outward. It becomes very easy to stop being curious and stop learning new things. Meanwhile, there are incredible ideas circling us all the time, but if our field of vision is very narrow it becomes impossible to see them. To get our creativity firing again we need to access these ideas, and the simplest way to do that is through…

CURIOSITY AND LEARNING

We need to begin to learn again. Learn something new. Something outside of our chosen field that will bring us new perspective.

But where to start? The answer is simple. It doesn't matter.

PICK SOMETHING

What you decide to study and explore is less important than simply starting the process of exploration. You need to light a match to start a fire. Curiosity and learning are like a dog chasing its tail. As you become curious you begin to learn, and the more you learn the more curious you become. It becomes an infinite loop, and this loop sparks ideas. Creativity comes from that curiosity: the burning desire to see what is on the other side and to find answers. But first you need to light the match.

JOURNEY

Think of it as an adventure. Where you start is just the first place on the map. Once you begin to walk and then run, the map will expand, get bigger and bigger. A whole new world will open up to you. The starting point is almost irrelevant. The important thing is to pick something and to start your curiosity and learning centre working again.

The **LENS**

As we begin to explore new ideas and disciplines, the lens with which we see the world will begin to change. Suddenly we can see layers of the world that we never had access to before. Having many lenses is the key to looking at our problems from different angles and perspectives, and to finding new, innovative solutions.

My friend Raphael Mazzucco is a fashion photographer and artist in New York City. A night out with him is always a journey through a maze of incredible places and people. Invariably, as the night wears on, the wine runs fast, and the conversation gets hushed, I am always fascinated listening to him talk. The world he sees is different than mine. He describes his world in relation to light and shadow, colour and shading. He describes a world that I can barely see. We look at the same scene but the depth of our vision is completely different. He can see in clear focus things that are almost completely veiled to me. His eyes have access to a different lens.

Our interests determine how we see the world. Those interests are pulled into tight focus while the rest of the scene is often blurred. Are you looking to rent an apartment? Suddenly all you see around you are "for rent" signs. Thinking of buying a new Volkswagen? Now, everywhere you go, VWs are popping up left and right.

The VWs have always been there, but without interest they are invisible. The world each of us sees is just one possible level of sight. One lens. To be more creative we need to open up to other lenses and other ways of seeing. The more we can see, the more ideas we can use in our creative work.

by
RAPHAEL MAZZUCCO
TAOS *2013*

The IDEA ACCELERATOR

A formal education is great. If you want to be a surgeon you are going to have to go to school. If you want to pilot a 747 from LAX to Tokyo, please complete the certification before you get behind the controls. I stumbled my way through a degree in political science while also going after a minor in modern dance (I'll save those stories for the next book), and I have definitely used the skills I learned in university in my creative life. But in this modern world there are many other ways to learn and become fluent in different subjects. If you want to get your ideas flowing again, to jump-start your curiosity and inspiration, you need to build an idea accelerator.

In 2005 the Internet was exploding. I was living in New York City and working on a new album. La Guardia Airport had become my second home, and I was commuting back up to Canada almost every weekend for shows.

While doing a festival in Montreal, I decided to reconnect with an old friend, Mitch Joel. Mitch is one of my best friends but we hadn't seen each other in a very long time. He started out as a rock journalist back in the eighties, but has since gone on to become the president of Twist Image, a large digital marketing agency, and he has written two bestselling business books: *Six Pixels of Separation* and *CTRL ALT Delete*. Mitch is in every way a "thought leader." At the time, I was fascinated by the Internet as I watched it radically transform the music business. After ten years of working as a professional musician, writing, recording, and touring, I had started to wonder what was next. I knew that music would always be a huge part of my life, but I also knew I wanted to expand beyond it and exercise different parts of my brain.

Mitch and I sat down at Shed Café on St. Laurent Boulevard. (Remember, this was 2005 — before most people had heard the word *blog* and before the existence of Twitter.) Over coffee, he laid out a vision of the Internet that really altered my thinking and changed the direction of my life. He ended our conversation with the red pill/blue pill speech from the movie *The Matrix*.

"This is your last chance. After this, there is no turning back. You take the blue pill and the story ends. You wake in your bed and believe whatever you want to believe. You take the red pill and you stay in Wonderland and I show you how deep the rabbit-hole goes. Remember — all I am offering is the truth, nothing more."

MORPHEUS *The Matrix*

We are both geeks. Obviously, I took the red pill.

THOUGHT LEADERS

The Internet is a double-edged sword. It can overwhelm you with useless crap: photos of cute cats and Double Dream Hands, or time-suck you into Facebook posts about friends and tweets about soup.

But...

It can also be an incredibly rich place: an idea-generating machine where you can learn almost anything. Never before has so much knowledge been available to so many people on the planet — so freely. The Internet is a learning game changer if you have the discipline to follow through and the focus to avoid distraction.

My idea accelerator started with Mitch's blog on digital marketing and business development, *Six Pixels of Separation*. Mentions of other thought leaders in his blog lead me down the rabbit-hole on an adventure through the Web: Clay Shirky, Seth Godin, Kara Swisher, Om Malik, Mathew Ingram, the Gillmore Gang, Tim Ferriss, Nora Young, Paul Kedrosky, Jenna Wortham, Avinash Kaushik, Kevin Rose, Joseph Jaffe, Sarah Lacy, Robert Scoble, Chris Brogan, Julien Smith, Guy Kawasaki, Fred Wilson, Kashmir Hill, Jason Hirschhorn, and on and on. A river of great ideas from really smart people. As you collect and organize more and more sources, a clear picture starts to emerge. You begin to understand the direction of the prevailing thoughts and ideas within that specific discipline. This collection of sources acts as an idea accelerator. It floods you with great ideas that can help spark your own. My idea accelerator for the Internet and tech looked like this:

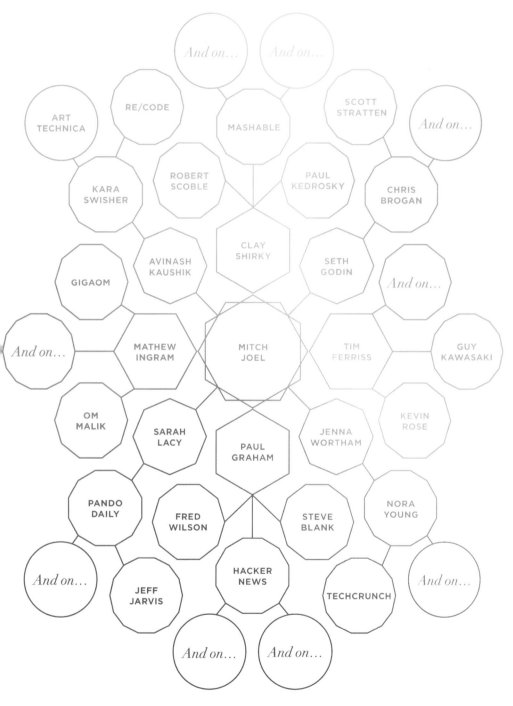

And on… And on…

ART TECHNICA

RE/CODE

MASHABLE

SCOTT STRATTEN

And on…

KARA SWISHER

ROBERT SCOBLE

PAUL KEDROSKY

CHRIS BROGAN

GIGAOM

AVINASH KAUSHIK

CLAY SHIRKY

SETH GODIN

And on…

And on…

MATHEW INGRAM

MITCH JOEL

TIM FERRISS

GUY KAWASAKI

OM MALIK

SARAH LACY

PAUL GRAHAM

JENNA WORTHAM

KEVIN ROSE

PANDO DAILY

FRED WILSON

STEVE BLANK

NORA YOUNG

And on…

JEFF JARVIS

HACKER NEWS

TECHCRUNCH

And on…

And on…

And on…

Before the Internet, getting this kind of information from thought leaders — people actively working at the top of their field — was almost impossible. The most you could hope for was a few books on the subject written years ago and a university professor that could outline some of the theories. Now we have access to the best people, talking about the things they are thinking about and currently working on while they are working on them. This level of access to ideas is unprecedented, and it's all just out there waiting to be read.

FEED READERS: REALLY SIMPLE SYNDICATION (RSS)
It has become very easy to develop hundreds of high-level sources for great ideas. But with so much to read it's also necessary to develop a methodology for sorting through masses of material quickly to find the gems related to your interests. For this I use a feed reader. Feed readers allow you to subscribe to a blog, journal, or web site, and organize category folders. Then, through RSS, the articles from the sites you have subscribed to are automatically syndicated into the proper folders. The feed reader shows you just the headline and the first paragraph of the articles, allowing you to scan through at lightning speed looking for items that spark your imagination. The other big benefit of feed readers is that they cut out the noise and distraction of the Web by showing you only the sources you want to see. Some consider readers to be an "old technology," but for me they are still the best way I've found to quickly track and scan through literally hundreds of articles from thought leaders in a very short period of time. RSS allows you to read the best of the best specifically connected to what you are interested in exploring. It's all right there online, free, and all you have to do is read.

EXPAND YOUR MAP

Once you start to get into this process of reading the blogs, articles, journals, and books of thought leaders, you will never be at a loss as to what to read next. It turns out that smart people know a lot of other smart people. And we all love to talk about our smart friends. One source will lead you to the next, constantly expanding your map.

Whatever your area of interest, you can now plug in directly to the stream of ideas that the smartest people in that field are thinking about.

ACTION

THIRTEEN

Start building your own idea accelerator. Find the blog of someone you respect in the field you are interested in exploring. Read. Add a new source each week. Read some more.

The point of an idea accelerator is not to make you an expert, but to flood you with ideas and get your imagination flowing freely.

REMEMBER

CREATIVITY IS
AN ACTION SPORT.
WE ARE TAKING

IDEAS

AND PUTTING THEM
IN MOTION.

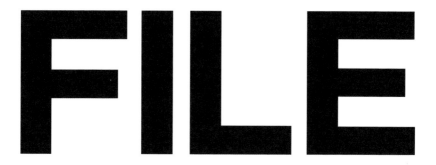

Reading is a great way to get your ideas flowing, but to make it really valuable you need to write as you go, and get in the habit of capturing ideas. You need to develop a methodology for filing ideas, first other people's and then your own. This habit of logging ideas is crucial. We need to pull them from the metaphysical realm and into the real world. Write them down to make them real. These ideas have now been taken out of the river of information rushing by us and have become part of our vernacular, part of our world. Through the process of writing, ideas become solidified within our subconscious and can more easily be called upon when needed.

METHODS OF FILING

There are many different methods we can use to file ideas. There is the old-school pen and paper. I still use this method for some things. I find it especially useful for songwriting (old habits die hard). I will use a new notebook for every album. There is something visceral about actually writing words on a page: the effort of writing, the physical act of the ink and the paper meeting the idea on the page.

For tech or anything Web, I like to use more modern methods. Today there are a ton of great applications that can help you file and organize your ideas. You can easily store web sites, photos, videos, text, audio, pretty much anything, and you can access the information on any device, smartphone, or tablet.

Experiment with different methods and mediums to see which works best for you. Old-school, new-school, there is no right answer. The most important thing is to find something that works, that you are comfortable with, and that you can continue to do as a daily habit. Write ideas down so you can call on them when they are needed.

Web and mobile applications are changing constantly.
To see an **UPDATED LIST OF THE TOOLS**
I'm using today go to letheelepahantsrun.com

ACTION

FOURTEEN

To form the habit of collecting and filing ideas, you need to be able to write them down wherever and whenever they occur. You need your system to be mobile. Get a small notebook or smartphone and keep it at the ready. Collect ideas when they strike.

Choose your poison.

*Experiment with different methods of filing
ideas to see what works best for you.
Choose your tools and then use them relentlessly.*

HUSTLERS
& THIEVES

You want to be original. One in a million. I get it. I do too. But don't be fooled. Artist or entrepreneur, in my mind we are all hustlers and thieves. We are an amalgamation of the ideas that surround us. There may be a few rare geniuses that can pull incredible brilliance out of the air without any prior knowledge or contextual influence. But for the rest of us, ideas are based on other ideas. We build off the work of others. Consciously or subconsciously, our creations are an evolution of the ones that came before.

We absorb and steal, rob and plunder — whatever it takes to get our creativity moving. We take the best ideas we can find, not to plagiarize them outright but to mash them together, twisting them into knots with the hope of exposing new shapes and new forms.

So hit the streets, hustlers and thieves. Steal and collect all the interesting ideas you can find, and then use them as the building blocks of your next great creation.

THE WAR OF ART & COMMERCE

There is a battle that rages in the land of creativity between the forces of art and commerce. The boundary separating the two is a line that all creative people flirt with and are constantly testing, stepping on, and stepping over. Countless hours have been spent over dinners and at coffee shops discussing and dissecting the eternal questions and conflicts of art versus commerce. Is your work too arty or too commercial?

What we are really talking about is creative intention. What are you trying to make and who are you making it for?

CREATIVE INTENTIONS SCALE

At the theoretical creative extremes are two archetypal creators. One is the "artistic creator" who is focused solely on self, with a purely internal vision and no thought for market or audience or sale. This creator is only concerned with getting his or her vision out, intact and "uncorrupted" by external forces. At the other extreme is the "commercial creator" who produces purely for the market with no thought, reason, or care for anything but what will please the audience and sell. For this creator, external feedback is a crucial part of the process. Polling, market research, and focus groups define the path and the final product.

Extreme artistic creators shouldn't be surprised when the world doesn't "get" their work and nobody comes to the launch. The work wasn't made with the world in mind. By the same token, pure commercial creators should not be shocked when they are not hailed as avant-garde geniuses, since their creations were made by committee.

Most of us fall somewhere in the middle, between the two archetypes. We recognize both sides and float back and forth, walking the path between the two, unable or unwilling to push too far in one direction or the other.

It is important to recognize that where we fit between the extremes is a choice and not an accident. Every day, with each tiny decision, we decide what kind of creators we are going to be. When I'm making music, I recognize that I care about how the music affects and is absorbed by the audience. I know they are there and I want the music to resonate and weave its way into their lives. At the same time, it tends to be solitary work, done alone or with a small group of friends, and we doggedly follow the thread where it takes us. Conversely, when we are building a new Web platform, like ArtistsforAmnesty.com, we are trying to create a unique aesthetic and user experience that is balanced, and often overridden, by the need to maintain utility, usability, and budget.

Different creative projects demand a different place on the scale of creative intention. Think about the part intention plays in your own creative process. It is only when you begin to view your place on the scale as a choice that you can begin to experiment and try pushing the needle one way or the other.

ACTION

FIFTEEN

Mark yourself on the creative intention scale

/ **1** WHERE ARE YOU NOW?   / **2** WHERE DO YOU WISH YOU COULD BE?

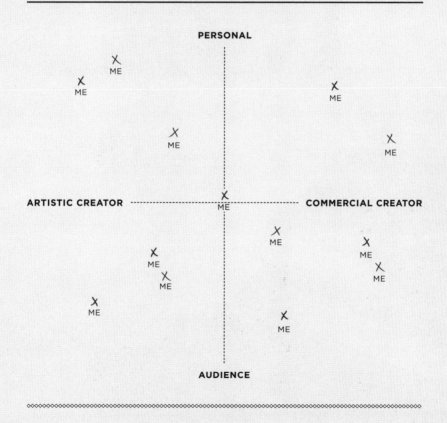

The IDEA ECONOMY

WHAT ARE IDEAS WORTH?

In the 1980s, if you wanted to protect your song and make sure no one stole your ideas, what you did was record a version of the song on a cassette tape and then send it to yourself by registered mail. Voilà, song protected.

I spent a lot of money on cassette tapes and padded envelopes. Looking back, this may well have given me a false sense of security.

Times have changed. These days, ideas are like oxygen — they are everywhere. The Internet has flipped the idea economy on its head. Now ideas flow like water on Twitter, Facebook, Pinterest, YouTube, blogs, torrent sites, Amazon, iTunes, and on and on. Today, value is measured by attention. Ideas still matter. You still need great ideas, but in a world where they are flowing so fast and furious and often for free, the real question is, can you get attention and traction for your great idea? In a world where everyone is a writer and a thinker, an Internet entrepreneur and a video producer, protecting your ideas becomes far less important than your ability to execute them.

"A lot of would-be startup founders think the key to the whole process is the initial idea, and from that point all you have to do is execute. Venture capitalists know better. If you go to VC firms with a brilliant idea that you'll tell them about if they sign a nondisclosure agreement, most will tell you to get lost. That shows how much a mere idea is worth. The market price is less than the inconvenience of signing an NDA."

PAUL GRAHAM *Y Combinator*

FILTER

I'm not the best guitar player in the world; in fact, I kind of suck, but I have made pretty good use of the eight chords I know. Songwriting for me works like this:

I sit down with the guitar and start to play.
I choose a random tempo and chord progression.
Strum or pick depending on my mood and I start to sing.
I improvise.
Melodies start to flow and words begin to emerge.
The sound of the strings, the rhythm,
the time of day, the lighting, the mood.
Ideas that I have been collecting, stored or written down over
the past few weeks, begin to surface in my improvisations.
Ideas begin to form: simple words or phrases.
I continue to improvise for five to ten minutes.
Sometimes I come up empty. But sometimes, a new melody
will marry itself with a chord progression and a turn of phrase.
Suddenly, I've found something new.

During this short session I will record ten different ideas on my phone and if I'm lucky I will keep one. I then email it to myself with the subject "song." I repeat this process ten to fifteen times a day. Later in the week I'll go back and listen to all the recordings to hear if I have anything good. Most get thrown out, but a few get put into the "good folder" and make it to the next phase. These ideas get worked on further to see if any of them will become "real songs." I define "real songs" as songs that get full lyrics and arrangements and may make it to the studio recording stage. When I first started in music twenty-five years ago, I would take a lot of "fake songs" all the way through the writing, arranging, and recording process, thinking that good production would make them "real" to me later. This almost never works. Over the years, as I have improved my ability to filter, these fake songs get dumped much earlier in the process.

NOT ALL IDEAS ARE WINNERS

You have to dig through a lot of crap to find the gems. Improving your ability to filter means you can move through material much faster and spend more time building good ideas and less time chasing dead ends.

I use the same filtering process when I go into the studio to arrange the songs. I can't read music. I can't play drums or bass. I'm a terrible piano player. I know very little about the violin, the cello, the trombone, or the trumpet. And yet, I am extremely confident and comfortable working with musicians who are virtuosos on their chosen instrument.

The reason is simple: What I am really good at is knowing what I like. I have spent a lot of time listening, and I know the ideas and sounds that spark something in me. I inherently understand how parts fit together. After years of study I have become a really good filter. I bring my musicians into a room and show them the song, usually a simple chord progression on the guitar and a vocal. Very basic. Then we start to jam.

I work with the band as a conductor, varying tempo and intensity looking for a starting point. Then it appears. As everyone plays I begin to sort through the sounds and the riffs:

"Keep that tempo"
"Let's try it up a half step"
"Keep the rhythm straight in the verse"
"Move the left hand higher on the keys
to make space for the vocal"
"Repeat the first half of that guitar arpeg-
gio but simplify the second half"
"Cello drops out for the first pre-chorus"
"Try playing the 16ths"

My filters allow me to sort through the flood of musical information washing over me. My job is to know what I like and what I don't, to be able to make quick decisive choices about what to keep and what to throw out. We work on a song for about an hour to see if something forms. I record throughout the session and email myself the parts that I think are good. Then we move on to the next song and the process starts again.

This practice of filing and filtering ideas is central to the creative process. It is important that you create a methodology that works for you, something you can stick to and can turn into an easy habit.

ACTION

SIXTEEN

Start developing a system
for filtering your collected ideas.

At the end of each week, go back through your work and review everything. Filter out the best ideas and start a new subsection or file just for them.

EXPERIMENT

You are a scientist.
You are looking for the answers.

Experimenting is a key component of creative thinking, and it happens continuously throughout the process. As you start to collect and filter ideas you begin to experiment with them. It's like banging rocks together, looking for the ones that spark. You don't know how two ideas will work together until you combine them. Creators are continually testing ideas and trying out different combinations to see what will "work."

You are a scientist.

But in your lab the elements are living and breathing. You have to balance out physical elements and ideas, but also emotions, feelings, and personalities. If you are working alone you have to battle your self-doubt and personal demons. If you are working in groups, personalities have to be managed and balanced. A thousand elements have to be filtered and melded together and then ripped apart again. The creative process is really like a cascading wave of tiny experiments, with the best results of each phase carrying us on to the next wave. It is never static and it is always evolving.

You are a scientist.
Embrace the experiment.

AND THEN OUT OF NOWHERE

AN
INSTANT
OF
UNDER-
STANDING

THE CLOUDS CLEAR AND YOU CAN SUDDENLY SEE

A MOMENT *of* CREATIVE COLLISION

The **aha** moments are when the light bulb switches on. This is the high of the creative process, when the ideas that you have spent so much time collecting, filtering, and experimenting with will finally pay off. You have discovered something new. You have a fresh idea you can build on and a clear direction for your journey. These are the moments that keep creativity addicts coming back for more. The moments of revelation, the small victories and precious discoveries are the lifeblood of the creative process. They make all the rest of the hard work that surrounds creativity worth doing, a million times over.

IDEAS COLLIDE

It was the year 2000 and Eminem had just released his song "Stan" on the radio. I was never the biggest Eminem fan — the misogynistic and homophobic lyrics were a bit of a turnoff — but I loved that specific song. There was something about it. The dark story Eminem wove and the way he skilfully integrated Dido's chorus to complete the sentiment. But what I especially loved was the undeniable drum and bass line that pulled it all together. "I want to make a song that grooves like that," I thought.

I FILED THE IDEA IN THE BANK.

During that same period, I was on tour in Europe. We were travelling on our tour bus through France and I woke up in my bunk with the flash of a brand new melody in my head. I scrambled for my tape recorder, desperate to capture it before it was lost. (The idea was born with the lyrics from lines 1, 4, and 5 fully formed.)

"Black black heart why would you offer more
Why would you make it easier on me to satisfy
Im on fire, Im rotting to the core
Im eating all your kings and queens
All your sex and your diamonds"

IDEA FILED.

Meanwhile, my friend Jeff Pierce was for some reason messing around with the "Flower Duet" from the opera *Lakmé*, and trying to build a sample that fit into a 4/4 time signature. Now, *Lakmé* was not normally a part of my musical vocabulary, but that particular sample sparked me.

IDEA FILED.

Back in Canada, in one intense writing session, these disparate ideas came together. The inspiration from the groove of Eminem's song "Stan," my new bus melody, and Jeff's mutant opera sample from *Lakmé* the Flower Duet.

A MOMENT OF CREATIVE COLLISION.

The song "Black Black Heart" went #1 in Canada and was top ten in fourteen countries across Europe and Asia. It went on to be covered by other artists in different languages, and despite the fact that the original song came out four years before YouTube even launched (in 2004), it still went on to accumulate over 10,000,000 YouTube plays.

And it all started with one flash. One light-bulb moment. But none of it, no part of this whole story would have happened if I had had that initial melody idea and just rolled over and gone back to sleep in my bunk rather than writing it down. Filing those ideas was the key to being able to access them later.

The moment of creative collision is just the beginning of the process. It is the flashpoint that marks the start of the journey, not the destination. The trick is to grab that one moment with both hands and then dive into the next phase of the creative process.

Listen to the song **"BLACK BLACK HEART"** *at* lettheelephantsrun.com

LET

THE

BE

THE WORK

"I am a great believer in luck, and I find the harder I work, the more I have of it."

THOMAS JEFFERSON

This is the other 95 percent of the creative process. It's the work, the grind, and the craft part. It's the part that wakes you up before dawn and keeps you going far into the night. It is the endless hours of thinking, planning, working, and revising. When you add this to the constant filing and filtering, the experimenting, the moments of creative collision, the development of a methodology, and the investment in the half-hour habit, suddenly it's easy to see how 10,000 hours can race by.

This is the part of the creative process that most people never see and never do. This is what it takes to turn a spark into something real. Something tangible. The ability to dedicate yourself to the work part of creativity is what will differentiate you from most of your peers.

**WILL YOU STICK WITH IT AND DRIVE THROUGH?
WILL YOU IGNORE DETRACTORS AND SOLDIER ON?
WILL YOU PUSH THROUGH ALL OBSTACLES
AND MAKE IT TO THE FINISH LINE?**

Successful creatives understand they must invest the time and do the work.

And that's it: Creativity is work. Wonderful work, but still work. You have to put in the time and push through the process.

From: 〉 Hide
To: David Usher 〉

No Subject
March 23, 2014 at 11:44 AM

Hey David

Here's a breakdown of the hours of work that went into making the painting:

Initial work spent stretching and priming the canvas (fairly mechanical work, but I do it myself so it's done right):..........3
Sketching out the idea (about 10 separate drawings):..14 hours
Time spent at home looking at imagery that contributed towards the making of the painting:...10 hours
Painting the painting (3.5 weeks at 7 hours per day):..126 hours
Grand total...
.......................153 hours

On top of these 153 hours there is general time spent "thinking about art." This would be really hard to estimate, as I'm thinking about painting while doing the dishes, etc — pretty much all the time! I don't think these hours should really be included as it would be impossible to estimate and also it's really who I am as a person — I love art so I'm pretty much always thinking about it.

I'd say this is fairly typical for most of my paintings — about 153 hours of work — although every now and again I do one that proceeds much faster. For example the one I just finished was painted in only 8 days. Conversely about once a year I find myself with a "problem painting," where everything goes wrong and it takes forever. I can send any more info you think would be useful — just let me know.

And hey, what about a night out, with the full gang next week?

best,
Kai

"Don't expect to write a first draft like a book you read and loved. What you don't see when you read a published book is the twenty or thirty drafts that happened before it got published."

WALTER MOSELY *Why We Write*

by **KAI McCALL**
I WAS ALRIGHT UNTIL
I FELL IN LOVE WITH YOU
2011

EXECUTION *is* EVERYTHING

Derek Sivers started out as a musician but went on to build one of the first successful Internet music start-ups. He founded CD Baby, an online music store, in 1998 and eventually sold it ten years later for $22 million. (It's worth noting, he donated all the money to charity.) In his book *Anything You Want* he charts out the value relationship between ideas and execution.

"To me, ideas are worth nothing unless executed. They are just a multiplier. Execution is worth millions... you need to multiply the two. The most brilliant idea, with no execution, is worth $20. The most brilliant idea takes great execution to be worth $20,000,000."

AWFUL IDEA	=	- 1
WEAK IDEA	=	1
SO-SO IDEA	=	5
GOOD IDEA	=	10
GREAT IDEA	=	15
BRILLIANT IDEA	=	20
NO EXECUTION	=	$1
WEAK EXECUTION	=	$1,000
SO-SO EXECUTION	=	$10,000
GOOD EXECUTION	=	$100,000
GREAT EXECUTION	=	$1,000,000

The ideas that form the basis of what you are working on are always important, but it is the work and execution that follow that will determine whether you succeed or not.

MOMENTUM

Poor Sisyphus. Pushing that rock up the hill is hard. Every time you start a new project, that is what it feels like. There is this immense initial excitement, but the finish line looks so damn far away. What you need is momentum. You need to get the rock rolling. While Sisyphus's rock always rolls back to the same starting point, our rock rolls down the other side and on to the next hill. Once you are in motion and start gaining speed, everything gets easier. Ideas flow faster, sparks fly more freely. Beware of anything that bogs you down and slows your forward motion. It can quickly drain you of your creative resources: money, time, enthusiasm, energy, collaborators.

If you stop, you exponentially increase the chances that you will never get to the finish line. Stopping gives your mind and body a chance to rest, but it also gives you time to consider all the other simpler things you could be doing. It gives an opening for resistance, for fear and doubt to slide back in and start messing with your resolve. If you stop, it takes an immense amount of energy to break the inertia and get the train moving again. When you have momentum, hold on to it. Momentum keeps everything flowing smoothly and propels you forward to the end.

**IT IS IMPORTANT TO WORK HARD BUT
IT IS MORE IMPORTANT TO WORK SMART.**

MAKE SURE
YOU LET YOUR
SUBCONSCIOUS

...

HASH PIPES
and HAND
GRENADES

What a night. Too much wine, too much whiskey, but great friends and crazy conversations. I got up at 4:30 a.m. to take a few Advil to ease the pounding in my head. By five I'm in the shower and the warm glow of the Advil has eased my headache and relaxed my body.

"Im too old for this shit"
"Today I start getting healthy, on the wagon, and no more red meat"
"I'm going to…"

Ideas start to flow. The hot water rushes over me and that wonderful river of ideas starts running. Connections appear and the internal dialogue begins as I trace out the path of the idea in my mind. I jump out of the shower, open my laptop, and begin to type. I capture the idea while it is happening. Before it has time to vanish into the ether.

When it comes to solving a creative problem or getting through a particularly difficult creative roadblock, working harder is sometimes not the answer. Connections and epiphanies do not always come through more work. In fact, if you are working really hard on a problem, sometimes the best way to get to a moment of creative collision is to do the opposite: go for a walk, work out, take in a movie, have a few drinks with friends. (I'm talking about short breaks — an hour, a couple of days — not enough to break your momentum.) Take your mind somewhere else and give your subconscious a chance to work on the problem.

The conscious mind is great at the endless grind of creative work, but the subconscious mind has a role to play as well. I am often chased out of sleep and dreams by ideas that have mutated in the night. My subconscious mind has connected ideas in ways I could never see while awake. It has drawn lines between disparate concepts that my active mind has failed to see. For most people, including me, daily hangovers and Advil are not a sustainable method for accessing the subconscious. So instead, I get up insanely early. I write every morning because while I am half asleep, before the real world has woken up, I can still access my subconscious. I can see ideas and connections that are not available to me once my "awake" mind takes over.

Work and discipline are important components for the creativity process, but sometimes you need to take a break, step back, and blow it all up in order to disconnect your active mind and give your subconscious a little room to breathe.

OPERATIONAL INFRASTRUCTURE

For most creators the time spent on the work of creation is the fun part. It's tough but enjoyable, with a little bit of suffering mixed in. Putting the paint on the canvas, designing the perfect user experience, or finding an elegant turn of phrase — these are all part of what we classically think of as the work of creation. These are the things creators dream about doing when they imagine their creative life. What they do not dream about is operational infrastructure.

Operational infrastructure consists of all the day-to-day business that surrounds the creative process. This is the grease that keeps the wheels turning — all the accounting, scheduling, space rental, promoting, production, and fundraising. These are the pillars that support the creative process. For anyone who wants to be a working creative over the long term, it is crucial to embrace the concept of operational infrastructure. Managing this infrastructure is the creator's job until the resources are found to have someone else take it over. Without this business structure there is no long-term creativity. All the successful creative people I know have either mastered these skills themselves or have a support team or patron who does it for them. It is very important not to confuse the intention of creativity with the business of creativity. One is a choice, but for most creators, if you want to continue to be creative over a long period of time, the other is a necessity.

My wife, Sabrina Reeves, has been an interdisciplinary theatre artist for the past fifteen years, first as one of the artistic directors of the New York–based company Bluemouth Inc., and now as the founder and artistic director of Fée Fatale in Montreal. Both these companies do work that often takes place outside of normal theatre spaces and mixes the disciplines of theatre, dance, music, and film to create truly unique work. This is not commercial work, but art that really pushes the boundaries.

So how do avant-garde theatre artists spend their time?

Creating in the studio, at rehearsal, on the stage, or on tour?

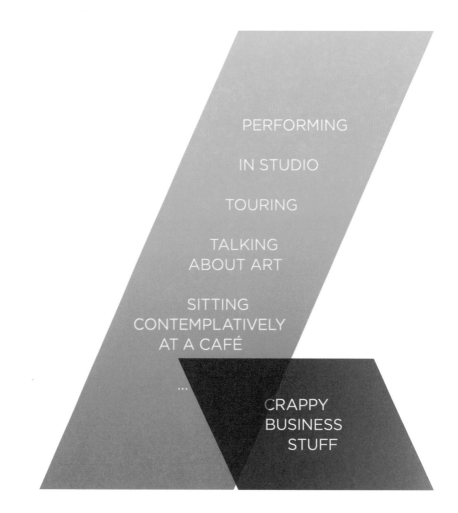

By osmosis, I have been involved in some capacity with almost every production of both Bluemouth Inc. and Fée Fatale — as labourer, loader, carpenter, musician, critic, or simply as moral support — so I have the inside scoop.

This is much closer to how the artist's life really breaks down. The business of operational infrastructure is not the fun part, but it is crucial to keep the machine running. Without it, long-term creativity stops.

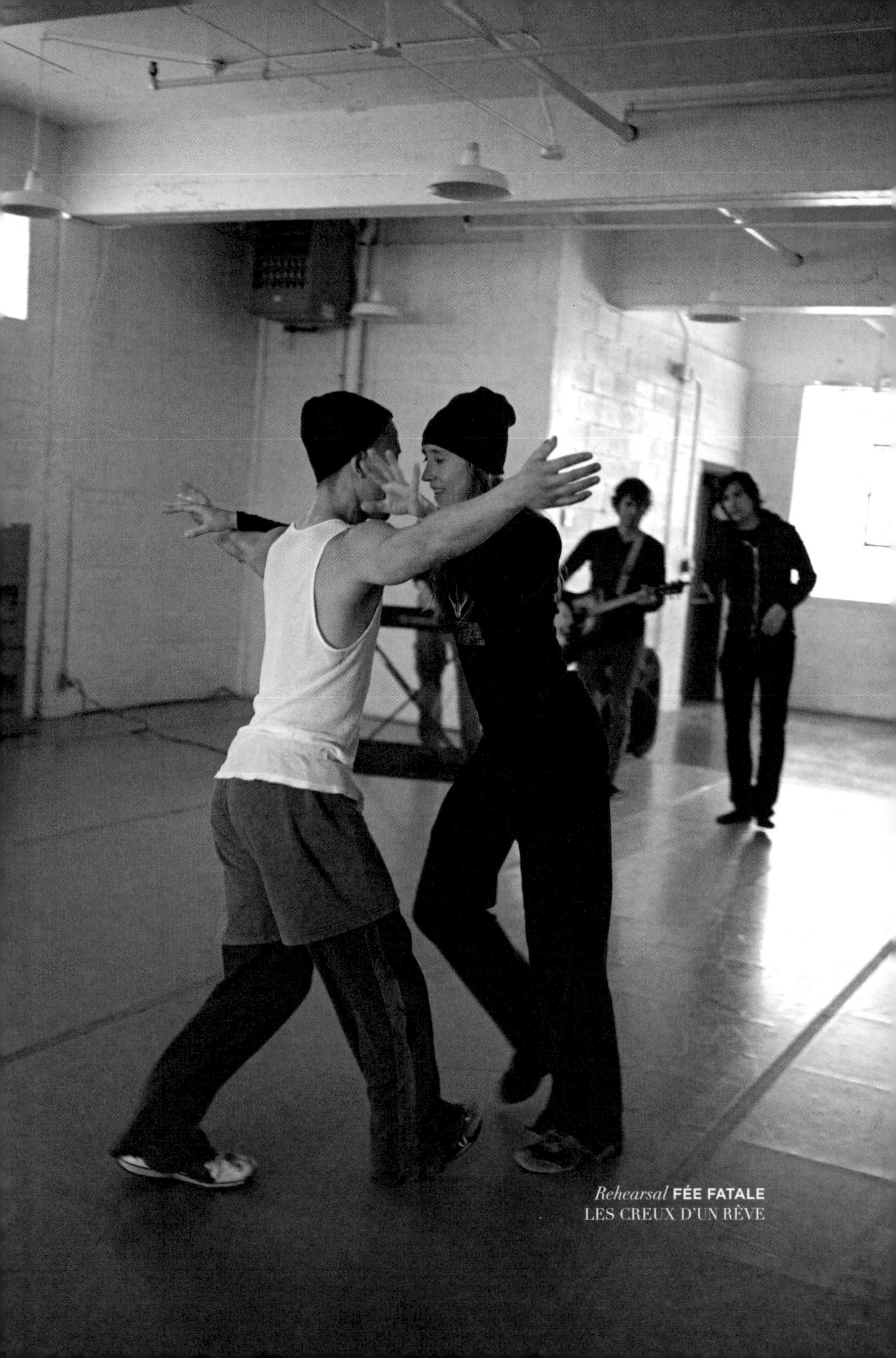

Rehearsal **FÉE FATALE**
LES CREUX D'UN RÊVE

BLUEMOUTH INC.
DANCE MARATHON

ACTION

SEVENTEEN

As a creator, think about your relationship to the business of creativity. How do you manage your operational infrastructure? Does it take up too much or too little of your creative headspace and time? This is something that is crucial for every creator to think about and manage. Use the space provided to outline your own infrastructure — where it is now, what is lacking, and what elements you need to improve upon to elevate your game.

_____

TIME:

SPACE:

MONEY:

ACCOUNTING:

PRODUCTION:

PROMOTION:

COLLABORATORS:

COMMIT

There comes a point in every project when you have to take a deep breath, step to the edge, and throw yourself off the cliff. You have to commit to the creative project and discipline you have chosen. It is important to tell the people around you what you are working on and be ready to take the inevitable wave of feedback, both positive and negative. Eventually, you have to stand up and own what you are making.

There are many reasons to commit and go public with your creativity.

TOUGHEN UP: IT'S TIME FOR FEEDBACK

At the beginning when ideas are fresh, they are often too fragile to stand up to outside opinion and criticism. They need the space to grow. But as time goes by and ideas mature and solidify, it becomes equally important to bring them out into the light and show them off. Once you have built up enough internal momentum and have started to gain confidence in what you are making, the roadblock of the friends and family factor can actually start working to your advantage.

Feedback always seems personal, and it's tempting to go into defensive mode and dismiss everything: "You just don't understand!" As creators we need to be tough. We need to put ideas into the world and be able to handle feedback without wilting, without becoming offended or angry.

When you make something public you get reflection. This reflection is incredibly valuable. You get a huge amount of data that can help inform your work and your process. Your job as creator is to filter all this information and use the pieces that you think have merit to make yourself better. It is also your job to reject and deflect the feedback that you think is not relevant, useful, or accurate. The hard part is filtering the good from the bad while simultaneously suspending the impulse to be overly defensive. Everyone has opinions, and it's amazing how suddenly everyone is an expert, ready to tell you what's wrong with your idea. It is important to filter feedback, but it is also crucial to filter the people giving it. Not all feedback is created equal.

MENTORS AND A TRUSTED CIRCLE

You don't want to be the smartest guy or girl in the room. If you are, you need to find a new room. To make your creative process better and become a more refined creative thinker, you need to get feedback from people who are better than you, smarter than you, and more experienced than you. You might not always take their advice. In fact, you may often reject it, but high-level feedback from really smart people makes you better, faster. It makes you think harder about the problems you are trying to solve. It forces you to go places you hadn't thought of. It makes you mount stronger defences for your work, defences that in turn make you stronger. Don't accept a feedback circle based solely on proximity — in other words, just because they are there. Your brother may be a fantastic guy but that doesn't mean he knows shit about what you're making. Search out great mentors and a trusted circle of people who can help elevate your game and make you better. Feedback is important. Make sure you are getting it from the right people.

The final reason to commit to your creativity in public is that it raises the stakes. It increases the consequences.

THE EGO FACTOR

It's much easier to fail or give up in the privacy of your bedroom. When no one knows what you have been working on, there is nothing at stake. It's much harder to do this in public, in front of your friends and family. When you commit to your creativity and go public, you dial up the ego factor. Creativity is hard, and there are many times in every process when we want to give up and quit. Sometimes the only thing that keeps you going is not wanting to admit failure. Your ego can be a great motivator when things get difficult. Ego can often push us through difficult situations where logic would have us lie down, give up, and do something easier.

ACTION

EIGHTEEN

Describe what you are working on in detail.
Define your timeline to completion.

Do you have a trusted circle?
YES ◯ *Show them your creative project and timeline.*
NO ◯ *Find a trusted circle.*

The EMOTIONAL ARC

Truth is, before every album comes out, I can be a bitch. In those intense few days before the release, before two years of my work gets put out there into the world, I'm a grouchy motherfucker. There are a million emotions flying around in my head as I anticipate letting go of my "baby" and the ensuing reaction and criticism. I am not the most fun man to be around.

The good part is that I've done this enough times now that I know what's happening to me. I have taken the time to write it down and I have a better understanding of how to handle it. These days, I don't go around yelling at everyone and everything. I go to a movie instead. I take those few days off because I'm preparing for what's coming.

"As a startup CEO, I slept like a baby. I woke up every two hours and cried."

BEN HOROWITZ *Andreessen Horowitz*

Just as there is a series of steps to each creative process that you need to define, follow, and deliver on, there is also an emotional arc to each creative journey. Putting yourself out there, taking risks, enduring criticism, doing something that your peers think is crazy — this is emotional stuff. Creativity is an emotional roller coaster with intense highs and brutal lows. Creators need to recognize that emotion is an integral part of the process and has a large influence on outcome. It's not only about how you manage the physical journey but the emotional journey as well. People are different and have many different ways of handling stress. Some people get incredibly defensive before they introduce an idea to a group because they fear rejection. Some people cry three-quarters of the way through every process because they are afraid to finish. Some get very aggressive and dominant when they are getting feedback and criticism about their idea. Just as it is crucial to write down and document the "physical" steps to your creative process, it is equally important to document your emotional journey so you can understand and improve on it each time. I'm not suggesting we should all be unfeeling Vulcans, but it is important to understand our emotions so we are not mindlessly dominated by them.

If you never document your emotional process, you will be forever destined to repeat it, unchanged, over and over again. If you write the process down, you will begin to understand the intricacies of your reactions and you will markedly improve your creative journey for yourself and everyone around you.

SHIP *it*

Shipping is the final step of the creative process. For me the value of an idea is only truly realized when it is delivered. Delivery could mean performing your site-specific interdisciplinary experimental dance piece to an audience of fifteen people in a barbershop or it could mean launching the next Google. When it comes to delivery, the key isn't the size of the release but the release itself. You need to get good at finishing and delivering to become good at creativity. Shipping something out to the world allows you to define the end point and allows you to move on in your creative journey.

SHIPPING IS WHAT FREES YOUR MIND TO THINK ABOUT WHAT'S NEXT.

Near the end of every project you can expect to feel the return of those dark passengers, resistance and fear. "This piece is shit." "What the hell was I thinking?" "It's not ready." So many creative dreams die here, right at the finish line.

So many unfinished projects wait in drawers, in closets, and on hard drives. They represent the stunted growth of their creators. The projects wouldn't necessarily have been groundbreaking or hugely successful, but their true value lies in the lost creative potential of their creators. Shipping is the key to moving on to the next adventure.

IF AN
IDEA
FALLS IN THE FOREST
AND NO ONE SEES
OR HEARS IT,
DID IT EVER
REALLY EXIST?

The MIDAS TOUCH

Not all ideas are winners. Not all projects are winners, either. Every project starts out with so much promise and hope. We push on, believing that we are making something amazing. When I am writing a new album I will file hundreds of initial ideas. Over the course of a year, about fifty or sixty songs will be pared down to around fourteen that will actually make the album. After a year and a half of work, I have run out of time, money, and patience. I ship it off. It's only then that I finally get to see what I've actually made.

I won't listen to the album again for about a year, until I've gotten some distance. Then, I put on my headphones and head out for a walk. The truth is:

Sometimes I love it, and sometimes not so much.

Don't expect everything you ever touch to turn to gold. The creative journey takes you through ups and downs, through winners and losers. It is absolutely normal to have creative projects that fail. Artistically or commercially. Failure is a part of the adventure. It comes with the territory. If you are a working creative at some point you will fail. The trick is learning how to handle failure when it arrives.

Will you wither and die? Or will you get back up?

After the inevitable pain-and-torment phase subsides, smart creatives use failure as a learning experience. They take all the relevant data from these experiences and learn as much as possible so as not to repeat their mistakes. Today's failures are often the basis for the next big win.

Think of creativity as a long game.

In the long game there are always incredible highs and devastating lows. That is the nature of creativity over the long term.

**PICK YOURSELF UP,
DUST YOURSELF OFF, AND MOVE ON
TO WHAT YOU ARE GOING TO MAKE NEXT.**

REPEATABLE

Here is some good news. Once you understand your creative process, and the steps that make it work, you can use that same system over and over again. Once you are really able to define your process it all becomes easier. Lather, rinse, repeat. This only works if, at the end of each cycle, you analyze what you have done, learn from it, and modify the parts that can be improved upon.

CREATIVE AMNESIA

Unfortunately, like with many emotionally intense experiences, we have an incredible ability to block out creative adventures as soon as they are done. It is as if the joy of finishing and the "birth" of our creative progeny wipe our memories of everything that happened along the way. We experience some kind of psychic break and can suffer from creative amnesia. We amplify the good parts and erase all the bad. We dive right back into the next process like it is our very first time, only to repeat our mistakes again and again.

> **"Those who cannot remember the past are condemned to repeat it"**
>
> GEORGE SANTAYANA

Post MORTEM

post·mor·tem / *adj.* **1.** Occurring or done after death.
2. analysis or study of a recently completed event

To break this cycle of creative amnesia we need to do a proper post-mortem at the end of each process. It is crucial to learn from each successive experience, to rigorously analyze past processes, and then to use this information to become better. If you want to develop a viable, repeatable creative formula, it is imperative to include a post-mortem in your process. Write down the good and the bad, the elements that push each project toward success as well as the ones that need to be modified or changed in future.

ACTION

NINETEEN

Did you do a post-mortem on your last creative experience? If not, do it now. There is still something to be learned.

Write a detailed post-mortem
of your last creative project.

DESIGNING
FAVOURABLE
Conditions

When I started this book I had my own case of creative amnesia. I forgot everything I had learned and I just dove right in, banging out words with no plan or thought to the process itself. I simply forgot to transfer my creative process to this new discipline. Instead, I jumped in like a newbie, ignoring all of my past experiences with creativity. That method led me down the path that most would-be authors follow: a general outline, a few chapters in a Word document, and, after two or three false starts, the inevitable realization that "It's too hard to write a book!" All over the world, on millions of computers, laptops, and iPads, there are partly finished novels and screenplays, abandoned and alone, just waiting patiently to be finished. Maybe you have one on yours?

The funny thing is, I know better. I've been in the creativity business my whole life. I have a ton of experience and still I managed to block it all out. I ignored everything that makes my process work and just decided to flail instead. To be successful with this book I needed to employ the elements that I always include in my creative process.

I always work with a team of collaborators. The nuts and bolts of the work is done alone, but for every project, from Web to music, I always have a trusted team of high-level co-conspirators to bounce things off, collaborate with, and who give me reflection. Reflection prevents you from living in a creative vacuum where you and your ideas just float, untethered to process. When I started this book I was floating. I quickly realized I needed to build a team to give me that reflection and feedback. I called my friend Hugh McGuire, who runs LibriVox, PressBooks, and is heavily involved with the self-publishing start-up scene. He introduced me to Oana Avasilichioaei, a manuscript editor. Oana and I immediately clicked and she became the first editor on this project. I would write and she would give feedback. I was no longer alone in a vacuum.

I felt strongly that if I was going to write a book on creativity it was crucial that the layout and design be inherently creative as well. I found it impossible to get a feeling for the direction of the book without defining the design at the same time, so to find a designer I began exploring the popular design portfolio web site Behance.net. I scoured the site for Montreal designers whose work seemed to embody the feeling and energy of the book I wanted to make. I then just cold emailed the ones I liked. "Hi, my name is David and I'm writing this book…" Through this process I found Caroline Blanchette. After a phone call and a quick meeting I knew I had found the right person, and Caroline became the book's graphic designer. I had found my team of collaborators.

To become better creators we need to fight through the creative amnesia and the natural impulse to "do it all by instinct." Knowing and being able to follow your instincts is a great gift, but being able to marry instincts with an informed process is what delivers you, project after project, year after year. It is what allows you to extract the creative knowledge you have built up in one discipline and transfer it onto another.

My team was in place and I was ready to start back into writing the book. But there was one crucial piece still missing. In any creative process,

I need consequences…

When I signed with **HOUSE OF ANANSI PRESS***, JANICE ZAWERBNY took over as editor.*

CONSEQUENCES

I wish I were the type of person who could just work. Put in the hours, day after day for as long as it takes. No deadline necessary. Just work till it's perfect. No one waiting. No expectations. All fun and flowers.

But that's not me.

Maybe some people can do it, but all of the working creative people I know need a deadline. We need consequences. We need to know that if we do not finish, if we do not ship by a certain date, something bad will happen. I said previously that creativity needs to follow the curves where they lead and needs to explore all the sights along the way, and this is true. But creativity also needs an end point, a finish line with tangible consequences waiting there. Without consequences, creativity can meander forever. It can circle like a ship without a rudder — a ship that's doomed to eventually sink. We need consequences to raise the stakes. We need to know that if we don't finish we will lose something: money, face, faith, or trust. Someone will be disappointed or disillusioned. People will talk and our stock will go down.

I have never been able to complete an album without the thrill and pressure of a deadline. Releasing an album is a pressure cooker. The record company slots your album into the calendar and the machine starts to roll — with marketing, publicity, A&R, agents, and managers all working toward that date. There is never enough time. Advertising buys and social media start pushing, focused on that one day. What the public doesn't see is the intense series of deliverables that lead up to the release. Drop-dead dates for the radio single master, album masters, artwork, et cetera.

My creative process needs the imminent release date, the line in the sand that focuses my mind on the project and really puts pressure on my creative self to produce.

When I started this book there were no consequences. No one was waiting for it and there were no expectations. I wrote bits here and there but there was no focus. To make my creative process work I needed to manufacture pressure and to construct consequences. When I built my team of collaborators, I also inadvertently began to build myself a new set of consequences. Suddenly, there were two busy professional people that were expecting deliverables from me.

PRESSURE.

I was forced to lay out my vision for the project in a clear and concise way that others could understand. I had to build a timeline. I had to lay out the framework for completion and start to visualize an end point.

PRESSURE.

I was also paying my collaborators for the work they were doing.

It's amazing how spending money quickly brings things into focus and raises your level of commitment. When you decide to start writing cheques you are also deciding to get more serious about your project.

PRESSURE.

	A	B	C	D	CR	DP
	Release Date	**Department**	**Day of Week**	**Weeks to Release**	**2-Oct-12**	
2	Contracts Done	Legal	Monday	15	18-Jun-12	
3	Artwork Discussion Begins	A & R / Marketing / Creative / Pre-Production / Legal	Monday	15	18-Jun-12	
4	All Tracks Licensed By	A & R / Business Affairs / Marketing	Tuesday	13	3-Jul-12	
5	Credits For Artwork Done	A & R/Creative/ Royalties	Tuesday	13	3-Jul-12	
6	Photo Shoot Complete	A & R / Marketing / Creative	Tuesday	13	3-Jul-12	
7	Website Design	Marketing / Creative	Wednesday	11	18-Jul-12	
8	Website Teaser	Marketing / Creative	Wednesday	9	1-Aug-12	
9	CD Pros	Marketing / Creative / Pre-Production	Wednesday	9	1-Aug-12	
10	Art Concept Done / Label Copy Complete	A & R / Creative / Royalties	Wednesday	9	1-Aug-12	
11	Censor Board Review Copies Due For Submission	Pre-Production	Monday	7	13-Aug-12	
12	New Release Information Due for Scheduling	Marketing	Tuesday	7	14-Aug-12	
13	Regular Sell Sheet Deadline	Marketing	Tuesday	6	21-Aug-12	
14	Advance Music Ordered	Marketing	Wednesday	6	22-Aug-12	
15	Parts Order Deadline	Pre-Production	Thursday	6	23-Aug-12	
16	Manufacturing Quantities Due To Production	Operations	Friday	6	24-Aug-12	
17	Parts Receipt Deadline - Special Packaging	Pre-Production	Monday	5	27-Aug-12	
18	Sell Book Solicitation Date	Catalogue Marketing	Monday	5	27-Aug-12	
19	Special Packaging Import Order Deadline	Production	Wednesday	5	29-Aug-12	
20	Label Copy In RMS	RMS Users (Various Departments)	Wednesday	5	29-Aug-12	
21	Censor Board Review Copies Due For Submission	Pre-Production	Friday	5	31-Aug-12	
22	Initiate Anti-Piracy Protection Plan	New Media	Friday	5	31-Aug-12	
23	Final Website Complete	Marketing / Creative	Friday	5	31-Aug-12	
24	Import Order Deadline	Production	Friday	5	31-Aug-12	
25	Finished Goods Ordered By	Production	Friday	5	31-Aug-12	
26	Parts Receipt Deadline - Regular Packaging	Pre-Production	Monday	4	3-Sep-12	
27	Audio Deadline for **Digital** (e-album and e-single)	Digital Services	Monday	4	3-Sep-12	
28	**Digital** Graphic Date (e-album and e-single)	Digital Services	Monday	4	3-Sep-12	
29	**Digital** Notification Deadline (e-album and e-single)	Digital Services	Thursday	4	6-Sep-12	
30	**Digital** Clearance Deadline (e-album and e-single)	Digital Services	Thursday	4	6-Sep-12	
31	All Components At Plant	Production	Monday	3	10-Sep-12	
32	Retail Order Deadline	Production / Customer Service	Thursday	3	13-Sep-12	
33	Deliver **Digital** file to Business Partners (e-album and e-single)	Digital Services	Thursday	2	20-Sep-12	
34	Finished Goods Received At Tapscott	Production	Thursday	2	20-Sep-12	
35	Retail / Pre-Ship (And Regular - When Available)	Customer Service	Friday	11 days	21-Sep-12	
36	Last Possible Ship Date For Product To Arrive At Retail For Street Date	Customer Service	Wednesday	6 days	26-Sep-12	
37	Promo Ship Date	Customer Service	Wednesday	6 days	26-Sep-12	
38	All Product To Be Delivered To Retail By	Customer Service	Friday	4 days	28-Sep-12	
39	**Commercial Release Date**		**Tuesday**	**0**	**2-Oct-12**	

TRANSFERABLE

**I use the same process to make an album.
The same process to make a Web platform. Same process
when I'm preparing a presentation for a business conference.
And the same process while writing these words.**

The creative process is not only repeatable but it is also transferable.

Creative thinking is transcendent. It can move beyond genre and discipline.

It is adaptable. Unfortunately, most of us are not. We have an incredible need to define ourselves in relation to what we do.

I AM A _____?

In order to make our creative thinking transferable we first need to be able to mentally divorce it from our chosen discipline. We need to be able to visualize our creative thinking as one thing and the discipline we work in as another. It is very common for creative people to intertwine these two concepts so tightly that they appear as one. We marry the act of creative thinking to the object of our creativity.

I'M A CHOREOGRAPHER
I'm creative in relation to dance

I'M A DESIGNER
I'm creative in relation to design

I'M AN ENTREPRENEUR
I'm creative in relation to business

When we do this, it makes it very difficult to really understand and define our creative skill set and then use that creative thinking in other areas of our lives. We marry ourselves to our chosen discipline.

Instead, try to visualize creative thinking as a language. Once you speak the language of creativity you can talk about many different subjects, not just one. You may need to learn some additional vocabulary for each specific subject, but you already speak the language.

I'm not going to pretend that each of us will be equal in every discipline. Interest and natural ability always play a big factor, but the ability to see one's creative thinking as separate from genre is one of the first steps to freeing up our creative process. An inadvertent side effect of this is that when you liberate your creative thinking from the discipline to which you have tied it, you suddenly free yourself to be interested equally in many different things.

When I tied my creativity to music, I was only interested in music and I could only use my creative thinking in relation to music. I believed they were bound together.

Once I realized my creative thinking was an autonomous process and not married to just music, then suddenly a whole new field of possible interests opened up to me.

Maybe the love I had for music could be found in many different places. Maybe it was more about the process of creativity than the specific genre. And just maybe I could use that same creative thinking and process in relation to all kinds of different ideas and situations.

When you learn the language of creativity it alters the lens through which you see the world.

The **PATH**

In many ways, the journey of making this book parallels the story within it. I started without any idea of how to work the medium of the book. I had many false starts and had to apply all my former creative knowledge to this new discipline to get it finished.

I threw myself in, got lost and overwhelmed. And then, I refocused on process.

EXPLORATION, COLLECTION, FILE, FILTER, CREATIVE COLLISIONS, THE WORK AND, FINALLY, DELIVERY.

The day I shipped out the manuscript was beyond scary and overwhelming, but win, lose, or draw, this book has already delivered me someplace new. I am a different person and in a different place than when I started. It has opened up all kinds of ideas and opportunities. The experience of making *Let the Elephants Run* has changed me and is already leading me to my next creative adventure.

**"Give me a sign,
Give me a reason to hold on
I'm holding on
What is a life,
a series of moments all in a line
just passing by..."**

DAVID USHER *And So We Run*

This is it. This is your life. The decisions you make every day, minute by minute and second by second, compile to determine how it will unfold. You get to choose what comes next.

Will you choose the safe path? The low-risk, well-trodden route travelled by everyone? Or will it be the curious life and the adventure of creative thinking? The choice doesn't need to be radical. Will you invest a little time each day in the pursuit of something new?

Before you pick, consider this:

In this new world, in this revolutionary time in our history, the old paradigms about risk versus safety no longer exist. The old world of stability is gone and the only thing you can be sure of is that the future will be volatile. For our jobs and our careers and our lives, change is the new normal. The path you choose right now, at this moment, will determine how prepared you are to handle that change when it comes knocking on your door.

Listen to the song **"AND SO WE RUN"** *at* lettheelephantsrun.com

WE ARE ALL
CREATIVE BEINGS.
WE ALL HAVE
A VAST, UNTAPPED
CREATIVE CAPACITY
WITHIN US.